Y0-BZT-580

THE COLOR OF EMPIRE

Issues in the History of American Foreign Relations

Series Editor: Robert J. McMahon, The Ohio State University

In this series

The Color of Empire: Race and American Foreign Relations,
Michael L. Krenn
Crisis and Crossfire: The United States and the Middle East Since
1945, *Peter L. Hahn*
Intimate Ties, Bitter Struggles: The United States and Latin
America Since 1945, *Alan McPherson*

THE COLOR OF EMPIRE

Race and American Foreign Relations

Michael L. Krenn

Potomac Books, Inc.
Washington, D.C.

Copyright © 2006 by Potomac Books, Inc.

Published in the United States by Potomac Books, Inc. All rights reserved. No part of this book may be reproduced in any manner whatsoever without written permission from the publisher, except in the case of brief quotations embodied in critical articles and reviews.

Library of Congress Cataloging-in-Publication Data
Krenn, Michael L., 1957–
  The color of empire : race and American foreign relations / Michael L. Krenn.—1st ed.
    p. cm.—(Issues in the history of American foreign relations)
  Includes bibliographical references and index.
  ISBN 1-57488-802-1 (hardcover : alk. paper)—ISBN 1-57488-803-X (pbk. : alk. paper)
  1. United States—Foreign relations. 2. United States—Race relations—Political aspects. 3. United States—Foreign relations—Philosophy. I. Title. II. Series.
  E183.7.K675 2006
  327.730089—dc22
                          2006014005

ISBN-10 1-57488-802-1 HC
ISBN-13 978-1-57488-802-7 HC
ISBN-10 1-57488-803-X PB
ISBN-13 978-1-57488-803-4 PB

Printed in the United States of America on acid-free paper that meets the American National Standards Institute Z39-48 Standard.

Potomac Books, Inc.
22841 Quicksilver Drive
Dulles, Virginia 20166

First Edition

10 9 8 7 6 5 4 3 2 1

For my daughters, Annaleah, Madelinne, and Summer, with the hope that the topic of this book will disappear from the world they will help to make. They make me proud every single day. And in memory of Joey, Dee Dee, and Johnny for making this world a lot more fun.

CONTENTS

Illustrations

SERIES EDITOR'S NOTE

FROM THE BIRTH OF THE AMERICAN republic in the late eighteenth century to the emergence of the United States as a fledgling world power at the end of the nineteenth century, the place of the United States within the broader international system of nation-states posed fundamental challenges to American and foreign statesmen alike. What role would—and could—a non-European power play in a Eurocentric world order? The combination of America's stunning economic transformation and two devastating world wars helped shatter the old European order, catapulting the United States into a position of global preeminence by the middle decades of the twentieth century. Since the mid-1940s, it has become common to refer to the United States as a superpower. Since the collapse of the Soviet Union, its only serious rival, and the concomitant end of the Cold War, it has become common to label the United States as the world's lone superpower, or "hyperpower," as a French diplomat labeled it in the late 1990s.

By any standard of measurement, the United States has long been, as it remains today, the dominant force in world affairs—economically, politically, militarily, and culturally.

The United States has placed, and continues to place, its own indelible stamp on the international system while shaping the aspirations, mores, tastes, living standards, and sometimes resentments and hatreds of hundreds of millions of ordinary people across the globe. Few subjects, consequently, loom larger in the history of the modern world than the often uneasy encounter between the United States and the nations and peoples beyond its shores.

This series, *Issues in the History of American Foreign Relations*, aims to provide students and general readers alike with a wide range of books, written by some of the outstanding scholarly experts of this generation, that elucidate key issues, themes, topics, and individuals in the nearly 250-year history of U.S. foreign relations. The series will cover an array of diverse subjects spanning from the era of the founding fathers to the present. Each book will offer a concise, accessible narrative, based upon the latest scholarship, followed by a careful selection of relevant primary documents. Primary sources enable readers to immerse themselves in the raw material of history, thereby facilitating the formation of informed, independent judgments about the subject at hand. To capitalize upon the unprecedented amount of non-American archival sources and materials currently available, most books will feature foreign as well as American material in the documentary section. A broad, international perspective on the external behavior of the United States, one of the major trends of recent scholarship, will be a prominent feature of the books in this series.

It is my fondest hope that this series will contribute to a greater engagement with and understanding of the complexities of this fascinating—and critical—subject.

Robert J. McMahon
Ohio State University

INTRODUCTION

IN THE ENGLISH LANGUAGE, the words for various colors can be used to create vivid imagery or an instantly understood symbol. A person can be "green with envy" or "beaten black and blue" or "seeing red." Black can stand for depression or, in the case of a black hat, the bad guy. Silver is the color of purity, as we all know, given those chivalric knights of old routinely suited up in armor made of the material. The success of a song or an album is denoted in its color: gold or platinum. And the songs themselves rely heavily on the imagery of color: Cream sings about a "white room," while the Rolling Stones urge us to "paint it black." Our language is a veritable rainbow.

In much the same fashion, colors have often proved quite useful and powerful in terms of describing the American empire. Sometimes it is green, the color of the money that drives it to intervene overseas and create international markets. And others it is red, the color of the blood that has been shed—by both Americans and others—as the cost of America's aggressive militarism. And let us not forget that red can be readily combined with white and blue, as a symbol of the nation's commitment to bring democracy, freedom, and justice to the world's people. Then again, America's empire might be as simple as some commentators occupying the extreme ends of the political spectrum have suggested: a black and white world, with the United States representing "good" (white) or "evil" (black). Other scholars attempt to stake out a middle ground, noting that international relations are more accurately portrayed as various shades of gray.

Yet, it might also be argued that American foreign policy—and the empire it has created—can be understood only when we consider a wider variety of colors. We must start with the predominantly white foreign policy making structures of the American government. Quickly, however, other colors enter the picture: the "red" Native American, the "black" African, the "yellow hordes" of the Far East, and those "little brown brothers" found in Asia, the Middle East, and Latin America. As different colors often do, these hues have sometimes clashed, sometimes complemented each other, and on very rare occasions, run into each other and created entirely different shades. When considered in such a fashion, the definition of the American empire as an "empire of color" becomes more understandable.

The purpose of this volume is to suggest the ways in which race and racism have come to play such an important role in American foreign policy. The literature on this topic has virtually exploded in the past few years, and it is the hope of the author that this book might bring together some of the most significant strands of thought contained in these valuable studies to create an alternative narrative of the growth of the American empire. This is a narrative suggesting that color—as much as economics, politics, and strategic interests—played and continues to play an important role in guiding and shaping U.S. relations with the world.

Defining different races has been a consuming passion for scientists, intellectuals, theologians, politicians, and others in America since its very beginnings and continues, in different shapes and forms, to the present. Human skulls have been examined for size, shape, and "cranial capacity." Human bone structure has been studied and compared to the skeletons of monkeys and apes to discern how far this or that race has progressed from its simian origins. Blood has been analyzed for consistency and color. Facial contours have been measured. Through all of this "scientific" hokum, however, one clear and easily definable measuring rod of race has always been the color of one's skin. And differences in skin color have very quickly evolved into skin color rankings—white being the most "civilized," or "progressive," or simply the most superior, with other shades arranged in descending order as they become "less white."

This focus on skin color as the primary determinant of one's race, and, more important, racial standing, explains the organization of this study. Chapter 1, "White," examines the development of the concept of race during the sixteenth, seventeenth, and eighteenth centuries. In particular, it looks at the growth of the concept of Anglo-Saxonism and how that concept was first transferred to the North American continent by the English settlers and then refined and reshaped by the American experience. In some ways, North America became a living laboratory for the development of racial ideas, as the Anglo-Saxon English came face to face with the "red" Native American and the "black" African.

In chapter 2, "Brown," those early racial constructs make their first forays into foreign relations. During the territorial expansion of the early to mid-1800s, the United States came into contact with Latin Americans, particularly Mexicans. The seizure of immense amounts of land from Mexico by force was justified very much on racial grounds. The "brown" Mexicans were simply not capable of properly utilizing the territory; it was up to the hardy white Anglo-Saxons to remove this impediment to progress—if necessary, at the end of a gun. Later in the century, with territorial expansion nearly complete, the United States turned to the acquisition of markets and resources in foreign lands. The Spanish-American War led to the Philippines coming into America's possession. The "little brown brothers" who inhabited the acquired islands needed the uplift and civilizing touch that only whites could bring. Through the tutelage of the Anglo-Saxon Americans, the Filipinos would become good people and good Christians—as well as good workers and good consumers.

In Chapter 3, "Yellow," we see the first serious challenge to America's racial empire. The influx of Chinese immigrants into the United States in the late 1800s and the rise of the Japanese empire created fears of what the "yellow hordes" of Asia would unleash on Western civilization. The Chinese found themselves excluded from America; the Japanese found themselves excluded from membership in the whites-only club of great world powers. When war eventually erupted between America and Japan, the result was what historian John Dower has called a "war without mercy," as decades-old racial animosities (on both sides) erupted into a violent fury. When the atomic bombs were dropped and Japan surrendered, the "rising tide of color" seemed to have been pushed back—at least for the time being.

Chapter 4, "Black," looks at the racially complicated post–World War II world through the triple lens of America's relations with Africa; America's efforts to cope with its own domestic racial problem, which attracted tremendous criticism around the world; and the African-American reaction to the Vietnam War. For years, America had been content to let the European colonialists take care of the "dark continent," but the Cold War and waning of European imperialism pushed the United States into direct contact with Africa and Africans. Though the Cold War compelled American officials to win the allegiance of the new black-ruled nations of Africa, the officials found it difficult to shed old racial and cultural perceptions, as demonstrated most graphically in the U.S. attitude toward the apartheid regime of South Africa. In addition, America found itself under increasing assault because of its own very visible racial problems. The civil rights movement and the white backlash against it attracted considerable attention in the international community. The Soviets instantly realized the propaganda value in accentuating the plight of America's black citizens, new nations in Africa and Asia became skeptical of U.S. claims to leadership of the "free world," and even America's allies began to wonder about a nation that could condemn the lack of democracy in Poland but looked the other way while South Carolina barred African Americans from voting. In response, the United States embarked on a number of tactics to counter these criticisms with less than stellar success. Finally, the Vietnam War, a war against the "yellow" man vigorously protested by the "black" man in the United States, served as a flashpoint that brought together many strands of America's racial empire.

The readers' initial reaction to the approach used in this volume might be to suggest that we are talking about ancient history. Many may argue that no one can deny that America *had* a problem with racism and that it was an unfortunate element of our society for many years, but that was so long ago. Perhaps it seems so to today's generation, raised on the rhetoric of political correctness, multiculturalism, and cultural diversity. Yet, it seems just yesterday that my father, mother, and I stopped at a Louisiana gas station because, as usual, I had drank far too much soda on the trip from our home in Texas and needed to make a bathroom stop. My father led me around to the back of the station where I found myself confronted with three choices: "Men," "Women," and "Colored." Born and raised in the South, and only eight years old, the color distinction was not what caught my attention. Instead, I was mortified that men and women would use the same bathroom and asked my father why the "colored people" got just one restroom. He did not answer immediately, and he did not look at me when he answered, "I guess that's just the way things are around here." The year was 1965—a mere forty years and eight presidents ago.

CHAPTER 1

WHITE

I N MARCH 1815 A VIRGINIAN TOOK up his pen to address a question that had been vexing one of his friends. The issue at hand was, "what constituted a mulatto by our law?" Legally, the matter was a simple one. A mulatto was someone with one-quarter "Negro" blood in their veins, in other words, anyone who had a grandfather or grandmother who was black. Yet, this writer had a naturally curious mind, and so he began to muse about the consequences of a mulatto mixing either with other mulattos, "pure Negro," or "pure white." It was no simple matter, as he explained.

> As the issue has one half the blood of each parent, and the blood of each of these may be made up of a variety of fractional mixtures, the estimate of their compound in some cases may be intricate, it becomes a mathematical problem of the same class with those on the mixtures of different liquors or different metals.

He proposed, therefore, that an "algebraical notation is the most convenient and intelligible" method of determining what constitutes a mulatto and how much "mixture" must take place before one was no longer considered a mulatto. After nearly a page of increasingly complicated equations, the writer suggested that a comparison with Merino rams might be another useful way of grasping the situation. A "fourth cross of one race of animals with another gives an issue equivalent for all sensible purposes to the original blood." Having dwelt on the subject in some depth, he concluded, "So much for this trifle."[1]

1

The modern reader must notice a disturbing scientific detachment in the above analysis, and who could believe that someone would spend so much time and effort on such an odious subject, then dismiss it as a "trifle"? For Americans such as Thomas Jefferson, the author of the missive, however, the issue of race was never a trifling one. Indeed, it was of paramount importance. Quite simply, for early Americans, race and color mattered.

The interest in race and color is of relatively recent origin. Of course, outward physical differences between various peoples have been noted since ancient times, with Aristotle himself devoting his intellect to trying to discover the reasons for these differences. Defending the idea of slavery, Aristotle argued that it was a simple case of those who were inferior bowing to the will of those who were quite obviously superior (and, he declared, benefiting from such obedience). He could attribute the physical differences between peoples from a variety of regions only to the influence of climate on such things as the shape of a person's head or the color of their skin. Biological factors did not enter into these equations, and the concept of race, as understood in its more modern usage, was virtually unknown.

In fact, some scholars suggest that the word "race" did not appear in the English language until 1508. Another 175 years passed before the next step was taken: using the idea of race to cleave humanity into distinct and very different categories. François Bernier, a French doctor, published a study in 1684 in which he described "four or five species or races of men." He drew his conclusions based entirely on considerations of differing physical features including general body and head shape and the color of one's skin. He also made no attempt at ranking the races from "best" to "worst" or "inferior" to "superior." Although Bernier's work earned him in later years the title of the inventor of racial classification, the publication did not have much impact on late-seventeenth-century society or science.

Given the nature of seventeenth- and eighteenth-century science, the fact that a study that suggested that different "races" of mankind existed did not find a ready audience is completely understandable. Science, to a large degree, found itself constrained by religious doctrines; any study that conflicted with those doctrines was generally dismissed or ignored. And so it was with any ideas about different races. The orthodox view was that God created Adam and Eve, and from that pair sprang the peoples of the world. The notion that there were other, distinct people in the world brought that assumption into serious doubt. After all, where had these people come from if not from the original couple in the Garden of Eden? This monogenesis viewpoint found itself scrambling to explain why, then, there was such a wide variety of peoples of different shapes and different colors around the world. If, for example, the earth was merely a few thousand years old, as most religious authorities believed, then how could even the vague explanation of climate be responsible for the very dramatic differences between human beings? Theologians struggled for an answer. Some merely announced that, as with so many other aspects of nature, the existence of various races was simply a mystery that the creator had not chosen to reveal. This was hardly a satisfactory answer, and so others looked to the Bible for evidence. Many latched onto the Tower of Babel story in Genesis. Here, God took a world of "one language" and "confused" the languages into many and spread the people across the lands of the earth. That explained, at least to some, how mankind came to be spread across the globe with different languages. But it did not provide a solution to the question of how and why those peoples had become so different in appearance. Or perhaps it did. In spreading his people around the globe, "confusing" their language, it was possible that God had other goals in mind. Perhaps, to punish the most blasphemous, the most sinful, he had "marked" these transgressors with different forms. Or, these sinners had been relegated to the most degraded and inhospitable areas where climate had worked its unhealthy will on these peoples. In any case, all this provided a way out of the quandary of explaining why people who sprang from a common origin ended up looking so different. And, of course, it suggested that despite the outward differences, people were people, each capable of salvation.

The first scientists to more thoroughly investigate race, then, were careful in their assessments as to the origins of the different races. Despite the delicate tiptoeing around the issue of monogenesis, however, the theory that there were indeed distinct races began to take hold more strongly in the 1700s. The Swedish scientist Carl Linnaeus became dissatisfied with the hodge-podge system of classifying and grouping various plant and animal forms and turned much of his career to creating more systematic and scientifically based taxonomies. In time, his attention turned to the human species. While he proclaimed his allegiance to the idea that God had created humans (and all other forms of life on the planet), he nevertheless found the physical differences between various peoples so striking that he argued that within the species Homo sapiens existed four distinct subcategories: Asiaticus, Africanus, Europeanus, and Americanus (referring to the Native Americans of the New World). Linnaeus was flirting with evolutionary theory with such ideas, but his argument that all of the subcategories fell under the species Homo sapiens *and* that that species was unchanging kept him largely free from any charges of contradicting religious orthodoxy.

Linnaeus, however, took his arguments about differences farther than many other scientists of the time. He suggested that these different subcategories also had different behavioral characteristics. Africans were almost childlike and lazy; Asians were greedy and lacked powers of concentration; Native Americans had hair-trigger tempers and could be incredibly stubborn. Europeans, on the other hand, were generally described in glowing terms: more civilized and gentle; terribly inventive and curious; and governed not by emotion or legend, but by laws. The scientist did not devote a great deal of time to trying to explain these differences, nor did he really have to do so. In many ways, his descriptions fell in with the Tower of Babel theory, in which the dispersed peoples had been marked by God and/or degraded by their environments. Perhaps inadvertently, however, Linnaeus had taken the discussion of race to a new level. He went beyond physical manifestations of that "degradation" and now ascribed characteristics of behavior to the various categories. And, he made those characteristics quite specific to individual categories. Finally, he clearly set up the European as the model, the standard of excellence against which all other groups must be measured—and found wanting. Quite simply, from the step of differentiating among the various "races" of mankind, Linnaeus had moved on to a rudimentary ranking of the peoples of the earth. And he left no doubt as to which people were on top.

Two other major figures in science took up Linnaeus's theories, tweaking and modifying them as they went. Georges-Louis Leclerc, Comte de Buffon, a French naturalist, compiled his findings in the massive *Histoire Naturelle*, published in forty-four volumes over more than fifty years. He was less certain than Linnaeus of distinct categories for the human race, but he did make clear that there were certainly differences to be accounted for. In large part, he attributed the differences to the environment—weather, location, food. Also, he seemed to agree with the Swedish scientist on one important point: the European race was the most progressive and most civilized of the various races when compared with the other groups. Buffon held out a glimmer of hope for these "degenerate" races: if they could somehow be transplanted to more hospitable environments, they could stop and perhaps even reverse the process of degeneration.

One of Buffon's contemporaries, German anatomy professor Johann Friedrich Blumenbach, expanded on Linnaeus's classification system for human beings. He maintained the same basic divisions for the Ethiopian (African) and American (Native American), but he disagreed with Linnaeus in lumping all Asians together, and so split this group into two categories: Mongolian (China and Japan, for example) and Malay (South Asia). Finally, instead of European, Blumenbach created a new term, "Caucasian," to describe the white race of Europe. Most of his reasoning for the different divisions emanated from his intense study of skull shape and size. In a rather unorthodox scientific method, he would stand astride a skull and look down upon it observing and recording its various characteristics in what would later come to be known as the "Blumenbach position." He also criticized the Swedish scholar for his "ranking" of the various groups. At the same time, he generally concurred with Buffon's description of the races beyond the Caucasian as "degraded." The Caucasian, he observed peering down at one of the skulls from his large collection, was the most perfectly formed of the various races. Indeed, he mused, human beings had probably originated in the Caucasus region (hence the name of the new racial class), and other races could be measured in terms of how far they deviated from this perfection.

By the late 1700s the idea of race and its place in the study of humankind was becoming solidly entrenched. Constrained by the religious and social mores of the times, few scientists were willing to step beyond the theory of monogenesis or to suggest that the noticeable differences between the peoples of the earth were more than a result of a poor environment or God's mysterious ways. Yet, with each study, each theory, the idea that there were in fact definably different races was becoming a scientifically accepted fact. All of the scientists tried, with varying degrees of success, to maintain the argument that all of these humans, different though they might appear, had originated from the same source and as such were members of the same species. Nevertheless, with every new observation about the "degraded" status of some races or about the perfection of the newly anointed Caucasian race, science was edging closer and closer to a very specific delineation of races from "superior" to "inferior"—and thus laying the pathway for modern racism.

To a large extent, science received a gigantic nudge in that direction by the exploration, discovery, and conquest of new lands by the European powers in the 1500s, 1600s, and 1700s. As adventurers from the Netherlands, France, Great Britain, Spain, and elsewhere in Europe fanned out across the globe, they found themselves confronted in much more direct and less theoretical ways by the "degraded" races described by Buffon and Blumenbach. Discovery might be accompanied by words about the "noble savages" they encountered in these far-off lands, but conquest (and attempts at Christianization) was usually accomplished by force and the savages—noble or not—were exterminated, enslaved, and forced to accept European rule. Race became a useful justification for these somewhat less than Christian attitudes and actions; inferiors, after all, did not have the rights of Europeans, and brutish barbarians understood only force. The very facts that the natives were usually so easily defeated and that European diseases swept through their ranks like a scythe were merely more indications of their weakness and inferiority.

The introduction of African slavery into the New World also had a powerful impact on the nascent theories of race. Race proved to be a sturdy support for the "peculiar institution." Slaveholder Thomas Jefferson, two decades before reducing the mulatto question to a mathematical formula and just a few years after the end of the American Revolution, concluded that Africans were a "distinct race" that could not, in his estimation, ever rise to the level of the superior white race. The importation of African slaves in the English colonies of North America, in particular, had another unforeseen consequence in terms of racial theorizing. Buffon, Blumenbach, and other scientists examining the issue of the different races had all come to virtually the same conclusion: the differences were the result of environment. Buffon had even suggested that the "degenerate" races, once transplanted to more hospitable climes, would begin a sort of regeneration. The African slaves in North America, however, steadfastly refused to regenerate. Generation after generation, even in the healthier climate and environment of the English colonies, they remained remarkably consistent in terms of color and general body type. This was a serious blow both to the idea of monogenesis and to the theory that the "lesser" races could, in time and with the right circumstances, shed their "degeneration" and begin their slow but steady climb back to civilization and respectability.

At the same time that the origins and status of various races were being debated and defined, the English began to evolve a more detailed mythology of their own beginnings. It drew largely from first-century Roman scholar Tacitus and his work *Germania,* in which he described the various tribes of German people. In often glowing terms, he detailed their history and social mores. In physical appearance, he declared, they were a "distinct, unmixed race, like none but themselves." While each tribe had its chief, the people as a whole decided issues of major importance. Their dedication to personal liberty and freedom was unbending. In war, they were fierce soldiers. In peace, they tended to their villages, hunted, and adamantly shunned any sort of intermixture with other tribes or peoples. (Tacitus did note with some disdain that the warriors, once the battles were ended, generally lived a life of unadulterated sloth, leaving most of the real work to "the women, the old men, and all the weakest members of the family.")

One of these tribes, just briefly mentioned in Tacitus's opus, was the Angles. The Angles were familiar to writers and scholars in fifteenth- and sixteenth-century England because they, like the Saxons, were among the Germanic tribes that invaded Great Britain in the fifth century as Roman rule of the island collapsed. British historians were content to argue that from the fifth century up to the Norman Conquest of England in 1066, the earlier invasion by the Angles and other tribes had resulted in making a new population called the Anglo-Saxons. As befit the rule of these Germanic sons of liberty, the period between the arrival of the Angles and the Norman invasion was viewed as one of unparalleled freedom.

It was not until the 1500s, however, that stories of the Angles and their arrival in England were of very great interest to anyone aside from a handful of historians and scholars. When Henry VIII shattered his relationship with the Catholic Church in Rome and established a new Anglican church, the Anglo-Saxons suddenly came to the fore. Since the English monarch was on somewhat shaky theological grounds for the rupture with the Church, his supporters quickly developed another line of attack by claiming that the Roman Catholic Church had become polluted and oppressive. Instead of a break with the real church, so they claimed, Henry's action was a gallant attempt to return to the "pure" English church and religion of the time of the Anglo-Saxons. It was a clever argument, though it is doubtful that it soothed any ruffled feathers in the Vatican.

It also opened the floodgates for a new, intense, and forceful interest in the Anglo-Saxon heritage of the English people. During the sixteenth, seventeenth, and eighteenth centuries, the English were truly aiming to discover who they were as a people and a nation. Thus, the 1500s were a propitious time to be looking for origins. The steady rise of the English to world power during those years prompted questions as to how and why they had come to be where they were. Heroic tales of the mighty Anglo-Saxons filled the void nicely. That the origins of the Anglo-

Saxons themselves were shrouded in the mists of time only added to their allure. Good mythology, after all, is always more appealing with a touch of mystery added to the mix. In addition, a lack of specific facts left English writers and scholars free to fill in the blanks and offer helpful interpretations.

The story of the Anglo-Saxons also provided handy fodder for contending political viewpoints in the 1600s and 1700s. For some, the arrival of the Anglo-Saxons brought with it a period of freedom and popular government unsurpassed in the history of mankind. The Norman Conquest threatened all of that, but with typical Anglo-Saxon stamina and strength, the English in the years hence had restored those proud traditions.

Writers such as Thomas Hobbes agreed with this interpretation, up to the point of the grand restoration of Anglo-Saxon ideals. Hobbes and his supporters argued that the Norman invasion virtually destroyed the Anglo-Saxon concepts of government. In an ironic twist, they turned the arguments that had been leveled against the Roman Catholic Church against the contemporary English government: from its pure Anglo-Saxon roots, it had become corrupted, arrogant, and abusive. This argument soon found a receptive audience among restless colonists in the faraway American colonies.

And so the mythology of the Anglo-Saxons bloomed. They were a restless, energetic people, constantly searching for new opportunities. As Tacitus noted, they were a people like no other—and they intended to keep it that way. They remained aloof from other tribes and peoples, seeing their intrusion as blemishes upon an otherwise perfect society. Their institutions—religious, political, and social—were as pure as the people themselves, and their government stressed the ideas of community *and* personal liberty. From the deep, dark forests of Germany, they emerged, pressing ever westward until they found the Promised Land—England, a place, separated from the petty squabbles of the European continent, where the Anglo-Saxons and their way of life could flourish. Some even suggested that there was a hint of fate, destiny, or even God's will in the Anglo-Saxon presence in England. Surely, the rapid success of the English nation was evidence enough that the Anglo-Saxons were a very special people indeed.

Simultaneous with the debates and discussions about races and origins, the rankings and orderings of human beings, the peering down upon skulls, and increasingly vivid myth making about people appearing out of the forests of Germany was the discovery and settlement of the

English colonies in North America. The basic outlines of the Anglo-Saxon mythology were already well-known to many of these American colonists, and they carried the racial precepts of their countrymen as they embarked on the discovery and conquest of the new land. Indeed, the transatlantic journey of racial and ethnic ideas formulated in England was remarkably smooth, and these ideas made an easy transition into the New World.

In the main, the Anglo-Saxon legend seemed to fit the American experience quite nicely. Like their German forefathers, the colonists had embarked on a perilous journey westward seeking new opportunities and freedoms. Almost from the beginning, the colonial experiment was often cloaked with religious overtones. If not everyone could agree that the new settlements would serve as "shining cities upon the hill," many colonists were content to believe that God's will was somehow behind the founding—and subsequent success—of the colonies. From a straggling collection of sometimes pitiful villages and towns, the American colonies prospered as the settlers carved a new life out of the dark and forbidding "wilderness" they confronted.

As the colonies grew and evolved, so too did the racial ideology they originally carried to the shores of North America. The reasons for these changes were both internal and external to the colonial experience, but by the end of the eighteenth century it was obvious that Americans had taken the relatively new theories of race and the Anglo-Saxon mythology and dramatically reshaped them to fit a new environment with new needs. First, and perhaps foremost, was the fact that the English colonies quickly became a living laboratory for testing and calibrating the dominant racial theories of the day. Whereas for British, French, Swedish, and German scientists, scholars, and theologians the issue of race was an intellectual puzzle, for the English colonists race and racial differences had entirely practical meanings. It was one thing to discuss biblical origins or come up with new terms for different people or dispassionately measure human skulls. It was quite another to come face to face with the "red" Native Americans and, later, the "black" Africans who were imported by the thousands to toil in the fields of the new colonies. These confrontations with different races solidified and hardened the racial views of the Americans in ways that no scholarly treatise could possibly achieve.

The Native Americans inhabiting the Atlantic coastline of the North American continent were the first "new" race to come under the gaze of the English colonists who had decided to make the New World their new home. The British arrivals were hardly surprised to find a native population. Stories of the indigenous populations of the Caribbean islands and the massive numbers of Native Americans found in Mexico were relatively well-known at the time. The natives found in North America, however, seemed different—less numerous, less settled, and (disappointingly) far less wealthy than the hordes of the Aztec empire. All of this made it a somewhat easier proposition to simply push the North American natives off their land, taking the territories and their resources for the use of the Anglo-Saxon invaders. And thus began more than three hundred years of depriving the Native Americans of their homes, sometimes by trickery and thievery, sometimes by "legal" treaties (which were broken or forgotten when it suited the interests of the English, and later American, signatories) or, if necessary, the application of brute force and virtual annihilation.

Simple greed for land and resources, fears for personal safety, and the Native Americans' sometimes less than hospitable reception of the colonists certainly accounted to some degree for the misery and death that generally resulted when natives encountered English colonists. Yet, from the very beginning, race also played a role in the new Americans' hostility toward the indigenous peoples. To be sure, the English occupation of North America was often accompanied by the rhetoric of "converting" or "Christianizing" the heathen natives they encountered. But as historian Thomas Gossett explains, "one must regretfully dismiss these efforts to convert the Indians as exceptions rather than the rule. Actual contact with the Indians seems to have engendered fear and hatred rather than the desire to convert."[2] A potent wellspring for that hatred lay in the racial theories developing simultaneous with the English conquest of its Atlantic seaboard empire.

Like most of their European contemporaries, the early English colonists were strict believers in monogenesis. Thus, their initial reaction to the Native Americans was that these were simply some of those unfortunates who had been dispersed at the time of the Tower of Babel. And some colonists believed that perhaps the natives' close contact with their Anglo-Saxon cousins would serve as the spark for regeneration. Closer contact with the Native Americans, intermittent warfare, and the constant English demand for more land led to the dismissal of that idea in a strikingly short period of time. For one thing, the usual explanations for the physical and cultural differences between the various races of mankind—climate and environment—seemed to have little relevance to the American experience. Certainly North America was a different environment, but not so uniquely different that it explained, at least to the satisfaction of a growing number of the English colonists, the "backwardness" of the Native Americans. If environment was really the cause of the "degradation" of the natives, then there should have been a subsequent *degeneration* of the English colonists. Instead, after some initial setbacks, the colonists thrived and prospered, turning a wilderness into a land of riches.

For another, the Native Americans, to a degree at first frustrating and then eventually infuriating, refused every opportunity to shed their degraded ways and cleave to the political, economic, and social customs of their new neighbors. Conversion, after all, was not merely the accepting of Christianity and Western civilization; it was also the forceful and permanent renouncing of one's heathen barbarism. As the years went by, however, the English colonists became hardened in the conclusion that, since the natives refused to do the latter, it was ridiculous and fruitless to attempt the former. The religious overtones of some of the colonial settlements, particularly among the New England Puritans, who believed that they were God's elect and that this land was *their* land (and not in a populistic, Woody Guthrie sort of way), only intensified the view that the Native American "savages" were a completely different kettle of fish.

Little by little, the colonial experience with the Native Americans began to erode the notion of monogenesis. How could the natives truly be the direct descendants of Adam and Eve? Climate and environment did not seem adequate explanations for the vast physical and cultural differences that were so apparent to the English colonists. The fact that closer contact with civilized people had no positive impact on the conditions of the natives only increased the suspicion that while the Native Americans might indeed be people, they were no long-lost brothers and sisters of the sturdy, progressive, innovative Anglo-Saxons. By the mid-1700s, no less an observer of the human condition than Benjamin Franklin would sputter that Native Americans were "barbarous tribes of savages that delight in war and take pride in murder."[3]

Most scholars of early America have concluded, however, that the massive importation of African slaves to the English colonies brought the issue of race to a sharper—and more menacing—focus. The Native Americans could be dispersed and pushed farther and farther away from civilized settlements; their racial inferiority, though widely accepted, became of largely academic interest to most of the English colonists (save those on the frontier who served as the sharp point of continued expansion westward). African slaves were a very different matter. They were brought quite unwillingly to the American colonies to serve as the arms and legs for the growing plantation economy of the South. Their numbers steadily increased, and unlike the natives, their function mandated close and constant contact with their white masters and white society in general.

The very "blackness" of the Africans was a primary factor in the generally disapproving attitudes of the American colonists. In legend and folklore, black was traditionally the color of evil and terror, characteristics that were easily transposed onto the African slaves, whose black skin bespoke their innate godlessness and unspeakable barbarism. Old folktales, however, were augmented by the scientific findings of individuals such as Buffon and Blumenbach. Both, to one degree or another, established white or Caucasian people as the paragon of humanity. Other races of varying hues were often ranked in terms of how far they deviated from that ideal. Africans, as the darkest of the dark, were therefore the polar opposites of the Anglo-Saxon whites. And, as the darkest race, it stood to reason that they must therefore be the most degraded of the races. All of this led to one unavoidable conclusion: that Africans must rank at the very bottom of humankind.

It did not take long, then, for the new Americans to ascribe a slate of unenviable traits to the Africans: childish, brutish, violence prone, barbaric, heathen, lewd, unintelligent, and sinful. The list was, in fact, relatively easy to compose, for all the Americans had to do was enumerate their many fine Anglo-Saxon qualities and then come up with the exact opposites to describe the Africans. Historian Gary Nash suggests that such comparisons served another purpose. With a "Puritan emphasis on self-control and the guilt over licentiousness which were widespread in England," the American colonists may have been "unconsciously projecting onto black men qualities which they had identified and shrank from in themselves." By establishing such a stark contrast between white and black, "the English were better able to convince themselves of their own role as God's chosen people, destined to carry their culture and religion to all corners of the earth."[4] And thus, as they had with the Native Americans, the American colonists began to slowly drift away from the idea of monogenesis. How, it was asked, could the Africans—so *very* different in such very important ways—truly be brothers with the Anglo-Saxons?

Even the American Revolution did little to change the colonists' basic racial attitudes toward the African slaves. Certainly the contradiction involved in having a people fighting for independence, liberty, and equality, while simultaneously holding other people in chattel slavery became apparent to many Americans. Yet, aside from some inspired rhetoric about true equality for all and a few isolated calls for an end to the institution, slavery came out of the Revolution stronger than ever. Partially, of course, this was the result of simple economics. The slaves were integral parts of the southern economy, and slaveholders had a substantial investment in their human property. But the racism developed over the last century and a half in the American colonies was also a determining factor. Equality, as it turned out, was not a universal ideal; when most Americans used the term, they spoke of equality among themselves and their Anglo-Saxon peers. How could a Revolution, no matter how dramatic, suddenly make equal what God and nature had seen fit to make unequal? The plight of free blacks in America, in which they faced constant discrimination and generally lacked all rights of citizenship, was an indication of what would face the much more numerous slaves if they were freed. As Jefferson wrote, free blacks must necessarily be "removed from beyond the reach of mixture." Better that they remain in slavery, where there was at least some opportunity for Christianizing the savages.

In addition to the internal dynamics of the meeting between white, red, and black, an important external factor also helped to shape the racist outlook that dominated the United States by the early nineteenth century. As with the mysterious Angles, it also came from Germany: Romanticism. The term is usually associated with developments in music, literature, and the arts beginning in the late 1700s. However, it was also a philosophical outlook on life. Most important for its ultimate impact on the growing views on Anglo-Saxonism, Romanticism accentuated the individual; more important, it suggested the unique qualities of individuals. An outgrowth of this thinking, Romantic Nationalism, posited that individual nations were formed by the unique qualities of their individual people. In some ways, this merely substantiated what the supporters of the Anglo-Saxon mythology had been saying for years: that the rise of the English empire (and the success of its American colonies) was the product of the greatness of its people. The accent on the individual, however, made for an important distinction, as Reginald Horsman explains: "The emphasis was clearly moving from institutions to individuals and races." Romantic writers and scholars "increasingly looked for ways in which individuals and peoples differed rather than for the qualities common to all human beings." Earlier interpretations of the Anglo-Saxons had always emphasized the strength and power of the institutions (forms of government, religion, and so on) of these Germanic warriors. The very success of the American Revolution—led and manned by the newer and

more vital strain of Anglo-Saxons who had carved a place for themselves in the New World—only increased the belief that the ideals and
institutions of the race (the *true and pure ideals*, not those corrupted and
embraced by the English crown) were superior to all others. Now, as the
eighteenth century drew to a close and the former English colonists turned
their attention to building and shaping their new nation, two centuries of
acrimonious relations with Native Americans and enslavement of Africans and the appealing song of Romantic Nationalism combined to
sharpen and refine views on race and Anglo-Saxonism. As Horsman concludes, "The way for this new myth was being prepared in the second
half of the eighteenth century; in the nineteenth century the Americans
were to share in the discovery that the secret of Saxon success lay not in
the institutions but in the blood."[5]

During the first half of the nineteenth century, blood—and brains,
and skulls, and skeletons—became of almost obsessive concern to a string
of American scientists and scholars. In some ways, they merely built on
the previous findings by European scientists during the seventeenth and
eighteenth centuries. Yet, their findings were also the culmination of two
centuries of the unique American experience with race and the product
of a fully developed Anglo-Saxon mythology superheated by the appealing strains of Romantic Nationalism. More so than many of their European peers, American thinkers on the issue of race began to lean toward
the theory of polygenesis, to draw more concrete divisions between the
races of humankind, and construct a more definitive ranking of those
races from superior to inferior. To the surprise and amazement of absolutely none of them, their studies proved without a doubt that the Anglo-
Saxon race (particularly its American branch) was at the top of the racial
pyramid.

Many historians argue that this scientific assault on monogenesis
was primarily a response of southern slaveholders to the sporadic attacks
on slavery. If they could prove that Africans were not simply different
human beings but perhaps an altogether different—and inferior—species, then any moral qualms about the institution could be rejected more
easily. In fact, however, a northerner led the charge. Dr. Samuel George
Morton was a Philadelphia physician who developed an early interest in
fossils and later served as the president of the Academy of Natural Science in the City of Brotherly Love. His fame as a man of science came
from his intense curiosity about human skulls. His rather macabre collection grew to nearly one thousand skulls, some that he collected on his
own fossil hunts, others that came from helpful scientists from around

the globe, and even a few that came courtesy of victims of the hangman's noose. With as much scientific precision as he could muster, Morton began his investigations into the cranial capacities of skulls representing the various races. His basic technique was to fill the skulls with buckshot or birdseed, and then measure how much of a given material fit into a given skull. For Morton, the matter was a simple one: a larger skull obviously held a larger—and therefore superior—brain. His findings remained consistent as he packed and unpacked his many human skulls. The largest skulls, by far, were those of Caucasians, averaging ninety or more cubic inches. The drop-off from there was dramatic. Asians, Native Americans, and Africans could barely muster eighty inches, with the latter two groups

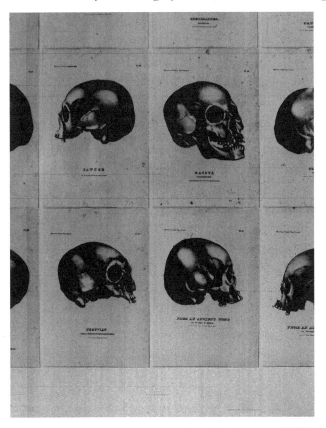

Drawings of just a few of the hundreds of skulls collected by Dr. Samuel G. Morton for his studies on racial differences. The collection was so massive that his contemporaries referred to it as an "American Golgotha." Source: Samuel G. Morton, Crania americana; or, A Comparative view of the skulls of various aboriginal nations of North and South America. To which is prefixed an essay on the varieties of the human species *(Philadelphia: J. Dobson, 1839), Plates 38, 39, 68, 69.*

jockeying for the position of smallest skulls.

With this hard data in hand, Morton began to draw a series of conclusions, many of which appeared in his two most famous works, *Crania Americana* (1839) and *Crania Ægyptica* (1844). Morton was one of the first to clearly state that the differences in the various races were most definitely not due to any sort of "degradation" caused by environment or climate. Instead, he suggested, the dramatic variations were evidence of multiple creations—polygenesis. Based on his measurement of skull capacities of different races from different time periods, he went on to postulate that the contemporary races were little changed, if at all, from the time of their origins. In short, racial differences remained consistent over time. Finally, his findings on cranial capacity led him to what he considered an irrefutable conclusion: Caucasians were the superior race, with other races ranking far behind. It was little surprise to Morton, therefore, that whites—particularly the hardy Anglo-Saxons—had achieved a position of dominance whenever and wherever they came into contact with people of color. It was altogether natural that Africans (the "lowest grade" of humanity) should be slaves to the commanding whites. In his volume looking at Egyptian skulls, for example, Morton overturned popular thinking about ancient Egyptian culture by declaring that the empire's ruling class had been white, with blacks in bondage doing their bidding. Caucasian rule over the inferior races, in his view, was part of a long and consistent history of the world.

Morton passed away in 1851, but by then a brash physician from Mobile, Alabama, was challenging his place as the preeminent American thinker on race. Josiah C. Nott was an ardent student of Morton's and eagerly absorbed the latter's ideas about racial differences. Nott, however, was possessed of an acerbic wit, a sarcastic attitude toward fundamentalist theology, and a deep and abiding wish to defend the institution of slavery. Beginning in the mid-1840s, Nott began his explorations of racial differences. His conclusions, which he expressed in no uncertain terms, soon began to move beyond the often circumspect findings of Morton. He came down strongly in favor of the idea of polygenesis, arguing that the different races had been placed where they were because those were the areas best suited to their strengths and weaknesses. The African, Asian, and Native American races had always been inferior to the Caucasian race and, in his opinion, always would be. These lower races had but one chance for advancement, and that was to mix with the stronger white race, infusing their weaker blood with the more powerful

Anglo-Saxon variety. He cautioned, however, that such mixing was in the long run disastrous for both races. Since he concluded that the individual races were, in fact, separate species, Nott argued that the interbreeding of species would eventually result in sterility for each of them. For the white race, the results were particularly horrendous. Its once powerful bloodline would become polluted, the progeny would become more and more degraded, and the Caucasians as a race would simply cease to exist. It was necessary, therefore, to prohibit any sexual contact between the races.

In 1854, three years after Morton's death, Nott produced his most famous study on race. His collaborator was an Englishman, George R. Gliddon. Gliddon fancied himself an Egyptologist who entertained

*Josiah C. Nott, coauthor with George Gliddon of the immense—and viciously racist—*Types of Mankind. *Especially popular with southern audiences, Nott argued that slavery was the natural state for African Americans. Source: Library of Congress Prints and Photographs Division, LC-USZ62-68007.*

American audiences with fantastic tales of mummies and ancient treasure found during his travels in Egypt. Gliddon was no novice in the world of race studies, having collected a number of the skulls that served as a basis for Morton's work on the cranial capacity of ancient Egyptians. Nott and Gliddon's *Types of Mankind* succeeded in finding the wide audience that Morton's own works had failed to cultivate. Weighing in at a ponderous nearly eight hundred pages, the volume nevertheless sold briskly and eventually went through numerous reprintings during the last half of the nineteenth century. To those who might wring their hands at the displacement and annihilation of the Native Americans or the enslavement of the Africans, the authors argued that the struggle between the races had gone on from the beginning of time. Indeed, "human progress has arisen mainly from the war of the races." Lest such a prospect sound a bit too frightening, Nott and Gliddon reassured their readers that the Caucasian race was well on its way to victory. The very fact that the English settlers had so easily routed the Native Americans from their lands was but one example of what awaited other races that stood in the pathway of the progressive Anglo-Saxons.

The notions of Morton, Nott, and Gliddon received a tremendous boost from an unexpected source. Louis Agassiz, one of the premier natural scientists of Europe, traveled to the United States in 1846 and eventually was hired to a professorship of zoology and geology at Harvard University. Although initially reluctant to accept the polygenesis position, the Swiss scholar was impressed with the work of the American thinkers on race. His personal experience with race also had a tremendous impact on his reevaluation of racial divisions. In a letter to his mother, Agassiz described his initial contact with the "degraded and degenerate" members of the black race in Philadelphia. Soon after, and having imbibed of the works of Morton and others, Agassiz moved to the position that the white and black races were most definitely separate species. In just a few years, Agassiz had accepted the rhetoric of Nott and Gliddon, even sending them an essay for inclusion in *Types of Mankind.*

By the mid-1800s the idea that mankind was not simply a collection of different "types" but was in fact made up of different species was gaining wide currency among both laymen and scholars in the United States. Mention of the idea of polygenesis still brought forth denunciations from some religious leaders, but even many theologians were coming around to the belief that perhaps God, for unknown reasons, brought forth numerous creations. Despite lingering disagreements over the origins of these species, a number of other points in the discussion of race were more tenaciously held. The myth of the Anglo-Saxon was now accepted as a virtual given, along with the notion that Americans were the newest and most powerful representatives of the Anglo-Saxon inheritance. The scientific claims of superior and inferior races also found an enthusiastic audience in the United States. They simultaneously explained the magnificent accomplishments of the American Anglo-Saxons, while justifying the elimination of the Native Americans and enslavement of the Africans. The theories of Buffon and Blumenbach, Morton, Nott and Gliddon, and even the renowned Agassiz established the basis of American thinking about race by the 1850s. The separate races were in fact separate species, each with a distinct and unchanging rank, from superior (Caucasian) to inferior (African, Asian, Native American). Mixture between the races would have catastrophic consequences, and thus the racial divisions had to be dogmatically defended. The displacement, annihilation, and/or enslavement of other races were not to be regretted. No apologies were needed. The constant—indeed, inevitable—advancement and spreading of the white, Anglo-Saxon race brought with it progress and civilization. Native Americans and Africans had already discovered this hard and immutable fact. Still, there were other races to be analyzed, measured, classified, observed, ranked, and, if necessary, conquered. By the mid-1800s race was far from a trifling matter for the American people, and they were ready to put their racial ideals to the test beyond U.S. borders.

CHAPTER 2

BROWN

I N THE YEARS PRIOR TO HIS collaboration with Josiah Nott, George Gliddon made his living in America by enthralling audiences with wild and exotic tales of ancient Egypt. Armed with several hundred "artifacts," Gliddon created a series of lectures in which he mixed his rather shallow interpretation of Egyptian history with his own racial theories about the natural inferiority of the black race and a passionate defense of the inevitability of the enslavement of Africans by superior whites. So it was, he informed the people who packed the lecture halls to hear him, with ancient Egypt.

In 1850 Gliddon attempted his greatest feat. Learning of the macabre "entertainment" of mummy unwrapping, which had become popular in England, he quickly acquired some mummies for his own show. More than two thousand people showed up for his lecture series in Boston when he announced that he would be performing the unwrapping of the mummy of a woman he described as the daughter of a high priest. It was a star-studded audience, with none other than Louis Agassiz in attendance for the finale. Science writer Heather Pringle, who has studied the bizarre "mummy craze" in the United States and England in the mid-nineteenth century, describes the event:

> In two earlier lectures, Gliddon had removed the princess's outer bandages in a kind of scientific striptease, tantalizing the audience while searching the linen for amulets and other treasures. That evening he planned on unveiling the princess in all her beauty. He sliced through the bandages and chipped loose the clots of resin. But as he tossed aside the last linen

21

strip from her loins, a loud gasp arose in the front row. The princess had a generous penis.[1]

The red-faced Gliddon survived the debacle in Boston, but his credibility as an Egyptologist took an enormous blow. He began to turn his attention more and more to the racial implications of his "scientific" findings and spent most of his remaining years in the South where he hoped he would find a more receptive audience. He continued on with his lectures and even performed at least one other mummy unwrapping. Most of his time, however, was spent working with Josiah Nott on *Types of Mankind*.

Gliddon's public embarrassment was indicative of more than simply the mix of pseudofacts and showmanship that often passed for "science" in nineteenth-century America. The fact that thousands of Americans, including some prominent people of society *and* science, flocked to his spectacles suggests an interesting and meaningful aspect of the American racism of the time. By the time Gliddon beat a hasty retreat from Boston following the unveiling of his Egyptian "princess," the ideas that the Anglo-Saxon race was one imbued with special talents and powers and that other races, ranked in descending order based on their color, were distinctly inferior were givens among most Americans. The notion that other races were considered inferior, however, did not mean that they were without a certain fascination for American audiences. The very fact that these various peoples were so obviously different made them instantly mysterious and even exotic; they were, in short, quite novel curiosities. Of course, Americans were also well aware that these human objects of interest were barbaric, savage, backward, licentious, violent, and cruel. As Gliddon discovered with his mummy "striptease," initial feelings of revulsion could be quickly overcome by even more intense feelings of titillation.

For most Americans in the mid-nineteenth century, much of the world beyond U.S. borders was like one giant mummy waiting to be unwrapped. The members of Gliddon's audiences generally knew as little of the inferior races and nations of their contemporary world as they did of ancient Egypt. Therefore, their knowledge of the Latin American tropics, the dark and forbidding jungles of Africa, or the mysterious Orient was acquired mostly secondhand, made up of rumor, legend and myth, and even, on occasion, serious scientific investigation. These lands and their people, which simultaneously repulsed and intrigued Americans, became of even greater interest as the United States expanded both its territory and its markets in roughly the last half of the 1800s. Certain of their own superiority, the same Americans who had no qualms about defiling the ancient dead for pleasure (and profit) began to tear away at the wrappings of other societies and cultures in their search for modern-day "amulets and other treasures," first on the North American continent and then overseas. As Gliddon and his audience of shocked Bostonians discovered, however, one could not always be certain about what one might find in these mysterious realms.

Throughout much of the 1840s and into the 1850s, the United States was gripped with a passion for territorial expansion. Journalist John O'Sullivan gave the passion a name when in 1845 he wrote of the "manifest destiny" of the United States to expand across the North American continent. To suggest that Americans hit upon the notion of expansion only in the mid-1840s, however, would be terribly misleading. From the beginnings of the English colonies along the Atlantic seaboard, the American presence had always been characterized by a restless, persistent, and sometimes violent push toward the West. Some suggested it was simply part of their Anglo-Saxon heritage, constantly pushing westward in search of new opportunities. Others argued that America's "destiny" had been preordained by a higher power (a belief that would be forever immortalized in John Gast's 1872 painting, *American Progress*, in which hardy American pioneers make their way across the western plains guided by a beautiful angel who floats above them). And some simply dispensed with pretense and declared that the United States needed the land and resources in the West.

Not surprisingly, American expansion had a racial aspect as well. Whether because of the pioneers' Anglo-Saxon blood or God's wishes or mere greed, the American movement westward necessarily meant that the occupants of western territory needed to vacate. Native Americans received the initial eviction notices and even the "civilized" tribes, such as the Cherokee, were soon sent packing. They followed what was romantically named, "the Trail of Tears" to the Oklahoma Territory, a trip that resulted in the deaths of an estimated four thousand Cherokee. For some, therefore, "American progress" came with an enormous and devastating price tag. Manifest Destiny became a handy catchall explanation to any who might bemoan the fate of the native peoples. Who, after all, would want to stand in the way of the nation's predestined power and glory? Certainly not President Andrew Jackson who, in arguing for the removal of the Native Americans farther west, declared in 1830,

> Humanity has often wept over the fate of the aborigines of this country, and Philanthropy has been long busily employed in devising means to avert it, but its progress has never for a

moment been arrested, and one by one have many powerful tribes disappeared from the earth. To follow to the tomb the last of his race and to tread on the graves of extinct nations excite melancholy reflections. But true philanthropy reconciles the mind to these vicissitudes as it does to the extinction of one generation to make room for another. In the monuments and fortresses of an unknown people, spread over the extensive regions of the West, we behold the memorials of a once powerful race, which was exterminated or has disappeared to make room for the existing savage tribes. Nor is there anything in this which, upon a comprehensive view of the general interests of the human race, is to be regretted. Philanthropy could not wish to see this continent restored to the conditions in which it was found by our forefathers. What good man would prefer a country covered with forests and ranged by a few thousand savages to our extensive Republic, studded with cities, towns, and prosperous farms, embellished with all the improvements which art can devise or industry execute, occupied by more than 12,000,000 happy people, and filled with all the blessings of liberty, civilization, and religion?[2]

Extinction and extermination were the fates awaiting the "few thousand savages." Weaker races gave way to more powerful races. For the next sixty years the United States routinely signed, then broke, treaties with various Native American tribes. In each instance, the American government solemnly swore itself to the protection of Native American lands. In nearly every instance, such promises lasted only until white settlers or business interests demanded access to the Indian lands. When "legal" means or outright bribery and corruption did not achieve the desired goals, brutal violence was brought to bear. The most infamous of the attacks by whites on Native Americans occurred in 1864 when a Colorado militia descended on the Cheyenne reservation at Sand Creek. When the massacre was over, two hundred Native Americans—many of them women and children—had been killed and many were horribly mutilated. By the late 1860s the American government adopted as its official policy the establishment of more secure—albeit smaller—reservations for Native Americans west of the Mississippi River. Again, thousands of Indians were forcibly relocated, and again, violence often erupted. In 1876 American forces led by George Armstrong Custer swept down on a Native American encampment at the Little Big Horn in the Montana territory for what they hoped would be an easy victory. Within minutes they found themselves surrounded and hopelessly outnumbered; Custer and over two hundred of his men were killed. Finally, fourteen years later, at a desolate spot in South Dakota named Wounded Knee, Custer's old military unit got its revenge when it confronted a group of mostly sick and hungry Sioux seeking refuge from the terrible conditions on their reservation. When the massacre was finished over two hundred Native Americans lay dead or wounded. With this, the "Indian Wars" were over, and Native Americans found themselves herded onto ever smaller parcels of the least desirable lands. Such was the path of American progress.

I

In the 1830s, 1840s, and into the 1850s, the path of American progress led westward and, on occasion, southward, which brought the United States into its first sustained and contentious contact with Latin America. There were constant debates and discussions about building a transisthmian canal through Central America, and that most famous of American filibusters, William Walker, led his band of mercenaries to a brief period of control in Nicaragua in the 1850s. Cuba was another piece of prime real estate much coveted by Americans (primarily slave owners looking to expand to new and fertile lands), but all of the blustering, threatening, and enticements that the United States could muster were not enough to compel the island's owner, Spain, to sell or cede the territory. It was Mexico, however, that came to be the focus of American expansionist efforts during the era of Manifest Destiny. Mexico had only recently gained its own independence from Spain in 1821. An immense republic situated on the western borders of the United States, it comprised not only its present-day territory, but also the lands that eventually became California, Nevada, Utah, Arizona, New Mexico, Texas, and parts of Colorado and Wyoming. Thus, for land-hungry Americans, Latin America proved to be a tempting target.

As with Gliddon's mummy, however, Latin America presented a spectacle that was at once alluring and at the very same time repulsive. American travelers, naturalists, and artists were drawn by the very backwardness of Latin America, its "primitive" lands, flora and fauna, the wild, colorful beauty of its natural surroundings. Many of America's most famous artists, for example, traveled to Latin America for inspiration in the years prior to the Civil War. Frederic Edwin Church produced some astounding landscapes. Titian Peale, his interest awakened by travelers' accounts, also visited the region and recorded his findings with sketches and paintings. The natives of Latin America also attracted attention. George Catlin specialized in capturing them for posterity. Martin Johnson

Heade visited a bit later, with his first trip to Latin America in 1863. He was fascinated by the foliage and specialized in detailed drawings and paintings of both the flowers and birds of the region. Some of these artists and many other Americans who visited Latin America in the first half of the nineteenth century were inspired by the travel narrative of Baron Alexander von Humboldt. The famous German naturalist conducted an extensive scientific mission to Latin America from 1799 to 1804 and later recounted his adventures and discoveries in a seven-volume tome published between 1814 and 1829. Humboldt described a nearly primeval world in Latin America, with vast regions virtually untouched by civilization.

Colorful birds, beautiful flowers, primordial wildernesses, and exotic animals certainly proved to be popular with tourists, artists, and scientists alike. The human inhabitants of Latin America, however, were quite a different matter. During the first decades of the nineteenth century, at the very same time that the United States was casting its eyes on the tempting lands to its west and south, Americans were studying, characterizing, and categorizing the people of those areas. Given the theories of race that had already been honed in the Americans' dealings with Native Americans and African slaves, it should come as no surprise that the "brown" people of Latin America, like the red and black before them, were found sorely wanting. Unlike the Native Americans and Africans, however, the Latin Americans had, by the 1820s, established independent nations, which, like the United States, had European ancestries. Yet, these differences as compared to other "inferior" races merely inspired Americans to delve more deeply into the racial and cultural makeup of the people to their south and west. One question emerged above all others: Why, with the infusion of European culture and technology, an apparent proclivity for republican government, and natural resources that seemed to beggar the imagination, were the Latin Americans so obviously and painfully behind their Anglo-Saxon neighbors in terms of creating wealth and powerful, well-managed governments?

Not surprisingly, climate and environment were cited as factors. As the debate on racial differences moved into the nineteenth century, this eighteenth-century idea that things such as the sun, temperatures, moisture, and so on could truly account for the dramatic differences in the human species began to lose steam. The theory did not, however, completely die out. Samuel Stanhope Smith, who became president of Princeton in the 1790s, suggested in his 1785 work, "An Essay on the Causes of the Variety of Complexion and Figure in the Human Species," that environment was the real determinant when it came to the "varieties" of "complexion and figure" among humans. He even went so far as to suggest that Africans who lived in less tropical climates for long periods of time would eventually begin to whiten. Smith republished his theories in a longer version in 1810, perhaps inspiring Dr. Hugh Williamson to put his own thoughts to paper a year later. Williamson had been one of North Carolina's representatives to the Constitutional Convention and had since made a name for himself in medicine and science. In 1811 he published *Observations on the Climate in Different Parts of America* (the rest of the title went on to take up most of the cover of the book). The chapter headings told the story in brief: "Different climates in Africa, Asia, and Europe produce men of different colours and features," "A black skin is fitted to a warm climate," and "Men are always found to change their colour with the climate."

While both Smith and Williamson relied on their theories about climate, environment, and race to defend the idea of monogenesis, neither man could refrain from offering opinions about the "darker" people found in the more inhospitable environments. Whether it was the red man of the North American continent or the black man from Africa, Smith and Williamson agreed that these "aborigines" were savage and degraded examples of humankind. According to Williamson, for example, the Native American was "unkind to his female" and was "attached to strong drink." Climate and environment, therefore, shaped the human race not only physically, but intellectually and morally as well.

Both scientists quickly realized the racial tightrope they were walking. If climate and environment did in fact lead to a degraded state of humanity, then what would happen to the hardy Anglo-Saxons who had determined to carve their new lives out of the American wilderness? Williamson flatly declared, "The human species do not degenerate." Even he must have been a little puzzled, then, by his argument later in his book that "There was a time in which the aborigines were much more civilized than they are at present." Smith took a different tack. He argued that the true difference between the Native American and African savages and the English colonizers was "civilization." For Smith, the "civilized" state from which the English came served as a sort of cultural sunscreen. Yes, their skin might get a shade darker and their features might become a bit coarser, but their innate adherence to civilization and all that went with it would ensure that they would not be pulled into a state of savagery and barbarism. In fact, Smith suggested, it might well be that proximity to the civilized whites might begin to rub off—to a small degree—on the Native Americans and African slaves.

Such theories transferred with relative ease to U.S. perceptions of Latin America. While in actuality the climate and environment of Latin America varies dramatically, most Americans who read the travelogues of Humboldt or saw the paintings of Church or Heade considered the region a tropical area, covered by dense jungle and inhabited by wild animals (and often wilder people). Given such an environment, it came as no surprise to people in the United States that Latin America (and Latin Americans) seemed to consistently lag behind its northern neighbor in development and progress. By the late 1800s scientists were coming to the conclusion that too much exposure to the climate and environment of Latin America (and other "tropical" areas) would actually work to enervate whites, sapping the willpower and vitality of even the proudest Anglo-Saxon. In such cases, the whites were said to have "gone native"—giving themselves over to laziness and licentiousness in the sultry jungle climes.

Latin Americans, however, had much more working against them than simply their natural environment. Their colonial heritage, according to many Americans, essentially doomed them to a future of backwardness and inferiority. At first glance, the argument seems odd. European invaders had conquered both Latin America and North America. But, as far as the English (and later Americans) were concerned, there the similarities ended. The Spanish (and the Portuguese in Brazil) were determined to be quite different Europeans. Unlike the sturdy, masculine, and self-reliant Anglo-Saxons, the Spanish were placed just a bit farther down the racial ladder. They were generally lumped in with other "Mediterranean" Europeans, such as Italians. Their closer proximity to the warmer climates led many English writers to tag the Spanish with the same attributes as the "savages" of the tropics, who were fairly lazy, quick-tempered, poor managers and planners, and rather effeminate (emotional, unstable, lacking serious reasoning powers).

Even the conquest of most of the New World by these "lesser" Europeans did not increase their prestige. In 1552 a Spanish priest by the name of Bartolomé de Las Casas published a searing indictment of the Spanish treatment of their Indian subjects entitled, *The Destruction of the Indies*. Soon translated into many languages, including English, the text became the basis for the so-called Black Legend. De Las Casas intended his treatise to serve as a plea for more humane treatment of the natives of South America, Mexico, and the Caribbean. Once English audiences found the book, however, it became a tool by which to condemn Spanish cruelty, greed, and incompetence in managing its New World colonies. Propagandists in Great Britain were soon at work creating even more lurid portraits of Spanish sadists who delighted in torturing and slaughtering the native inhabitants of the lands they invaded. Instead of developing the regions and bringing civilization to them, the Spanish conquistadors spent their time inflicting suffering, raping, and pillaging. Such stories worked nicely when contrasted with the industrious, profitable, and orderly English colonies in North America. (The slaughter of the North American natives and enslavement of Africans were issues conveniently omitted from these tales.)

The Spanish also brought with them two institutions that, at least according to the English (and, later, Americans), sealed the fate of the region in terms of progress and development. The first was the monarchy. The English also had a monarchy, of course, but their Anglo-Saxon heritage meant that it was quite different from the Spanish variety. The Spanish kings and queens (who were usually characterized as the "Mediterranean" branch of the European family tree) were generally thought a pretty sorry lot—greedy, corrupt, dissipated, and none too bright. Furthermore, the Spanish royalty ruled with an authoritarianism that appalled English observers. While the democratic-minded Anglo-Saxons created what amounted to a constitutional monarchy, the Spanish rulers had become tyrants and autocrats. Such, at least, was the view espoused in the ever-expanding Black Legend. What this all meant for Latin America was clear. Instead of creating societies in which men (not women—even the "democratic" American settlers would not go that far) determined their own fates and built institutions for self-governance, the Latin Americans lived under the absolute authority of the king and brute force was the preferred method of gaining obedience and loyalty.

Adding to the servile nature of the Latin Americans was the second Spanish import—the Catholic Church. Anti-Catholicism was a powerful and widespread force in early America and lasted well into the twentieth century. The mostly Protestant population of the English colonies found Catholicism to be an odious and repulsive institution. Fantastic tales arose about orgies between priests and nuns, black magic rituals, and the murder and sacrifice of young children. The Church's close connection to some of the most autocratic regimes in Europe (Spain and France, for example) merely cemented the idea that it was an authoritarian pseudogovernment masquerading as a religion. As with the Spanish monarchy, the dictatorial nature of Catholicism and the pope who stood at its head led to a state of near-slavery for the people who were forced to march to its dogmas. Thomas Jefferson, writing to Alexander von Humboldt in 1813, spoke for many of his fellow Americans when he declared, "History, I believe, furnishes no example of a priest-ridden people maintaining a free civil government. This marks the lowest grade of ignorance, of which their civil as well as religious leaders will always avail themselves for their own purposes."

In spite of the rigorously authoritarian rule the Spanish inflicted on their Latin American colonies, it was the laxness of the Spanish in one particular area that caused the greatest concern among American observers. In the English colonies, the Anglo-Saxon settlers insisted on remaining aloof from other races. So, in the English settlements, and in the American states that followed, a strict separation of the races was observed. It was not uncommon for white men to have sexual relations with Native American women, but the practice was always frowned upon. In the South, the growing numbers of mulatto children attested to the not infrequent liaisons between masters and slaves. Officially, however, miscegenation was at first deemed immoral and then was eventually designated as illegal. All of this was hardly surprising, for what upstanding Anglo-Saxon would want to weaken the bloodlines by siring "mixed" progeny?

The Spanish rulers of Latin America, however, seemed to have no such qualms about the mixing of the races. To the disgust and then the horror of the English and Americans, the Spanish showed surprisingly little concern as Native American mixed with Spanish, Spanish mixed with African, and African mixed with Native American. Indeed, the bloodlines became so confusing that it is doubtful that even Jefferson's algebraic equations could bring order to the chaos. The Spanish themselves soon developed a dizzying variety of terms to describe the various combinations of races. The very fact that they did so, however, was merely proof to their English and American neighbors that race mixing in Latin America had reached truly catastrophic levels. The deleterious consequences of any mixing of the races was patently evident to Josiah Nott, who wrote in his 1842 study of mulattos, "wherever in the history of the world the inferior races have been conquered and mixed in with the Caucasian, the latter have sunk into barbarism." Louis Agassiz, traveling to Brazil just after the American Civil War, expressed what many leading thinkers on the idea of race believed when he bemoaned "the enfeebled character of the population" in the gigantic Latin American nation. He concluded that one could not "deny the deterioration consequent upon an amalgamation of races, more widespread here than in any other country in the world, and which is rapidly effacing the best qualities of the white man, the negro, and the Indian, leaving a mongrel nondescript type, deficient in physical and mental energy."

Nott, in his writings, suggested that such "interbreeding" resulted in sterility and an inability to reproduce. What Agassiz and others posited, however, was something quite different. The term "mongrel" appeared more and more often to describe the resulting progeny in Latin America. Yet, it was not simply that the blood of Native Americans, Africans, and Spaniards were mixing together in confusing and morally repugnant ways. As Agassiz bluntly declared, such mixtures were "rapidly effacing the best qualities" of all three races involved. What he and other men of science believed was that in the mixture of racial bloods the very worst qualities of each race would be evident in the resulting children. Thus, in Latin America, generations of miscegenation between the three races had produced human specimens exhibiting the laziness, effeminacy, and violence of the Spanish; the brutishness, indolence, and licentiousness of the African; and the cowardice, backwardness, and savagery of the Native American. The combination was not pleasant, but it was one that fit in with the overall view in the United States concerning their neighbors to the south. Given the enervating climate, the murderous legacy of the Black Legend, the slavish devotion to Catholicism, and the deterioration of all races involved through a lax attitude toward race mixing, was it any surprise that Latin America languished in poverty, despotism, and societies that bordered on barbaric? Hardworking, Protestant, Anglo-Saxon sons of England could only shake their heads—and muse about how much more profitable and civilized such lands would be in their own white hands.

Such were the perceptions of Latin America and its people held by most of the tens of thousands of Americans who flooded into Texas in the 1820s and early 1830s. The vast territory of Texas was then a part of Mexico, which had gained its independence from Spain in 1821. To the surprise of many people on both sides of the border, the Mexican government allowed, and even encouraged, the immigration of Americans into its thinly populated lands north of the Rio Grande. For Mexico, the decision was practical. The Americans had already shown themselves to be incredibly land hungry—the Louisiana Purchase and the acquisition of Florida suggested as much. And there was no denying that the United States already had its eyes on the massive territories to its west, most of the land controlled by the newly independent nation of Mexico. In addition, these territories were very sparsely populated, and attacks by Native Americans on the few settlers were a frequent occurrence. Mexican officials hoped that inviting Americans to live in and develop these areas would serve multiple purposes: provide a bulwark against Native Americans, turn empty areas into thriving (and tax-producing) settlements, and forestall U.S. acquisition of the regions (since the American settlers were made to give oaths that they would convert to Catholicism and become Mexican citizens). However, from the Mexican viewpoint, the experiment soon proved to be a miserable and costly failure.

Although the Mexican government did not vigorously push Catholicism on the American settlers, it still rankled the Protestant Anglo-Saxons that they lived in a Catholic society. In addition, Mexico prohibited slavery. The Mexican government usually turned a blind eye to the fact that many of the American settlers brought slaves with them, but the knowledge that their "property" might be threatened or seized at some time in the future disturbed the new Texans. As troubling as the religion and politics of the host nation were, the Mexicans themselves elicited the most concern and criticism from the Americans. In line with the general thinking about Latin Americans, the Mexicans were viewed as a "mongrel" race, which had inherited the very worst characteristics of the Spanish, Native American, and African blood. Thus, the "typical" Mexican was lazy, backward, dirty, childlike, vicious, immoral, and incapable of self-improvement. One of the settlers, Sam Houston, declared, "The vigor of the descendants of the sturdy north will never mix with the phlegm of the indolent Mexicans, no matter how long we may live among them." Stephen Austin, one of the earliest leaders of American immigration to Mexico, was more direct when he described the Mexican people as "bigoted and superstitious to an extreem [*sic*], and indolence appears to be the general order of the day. . . . To be candid the majority of the whole nation as far as I have seen them want nothing but tails to be more brutes than the apes."[3]

It did not take long for such animus to boil over into contention with Mexican officials. In 1830 Mexico closed its borders to further American immigration (though thousands continued to sneak through illegally). By late 1835 fighting had broken out between the American settlers and Mexicans, and the Texas Revolution had begun. The Americans made clear their reasons for revolt in numerous petitions and proclamations. As one noted, "The Anglo-Americans and the Mexicans, if not primitively a different people, habit, education and religion, have made them essentially so. The two different people cannot mingle together. The strong prejudices that existed at the first emigrations, so far from having become softened and neutralised contact, having increased many fold. And as long as the people of Texas belong to the Mexican nation, their interests will be jeopardized, and their prosperity cramped."[4] In just a few months, following the stand of the Texans at the Battle of the Alamo, the army of Mexico was defeated and Texas became an independent republic.

By the mid-1840s America was under the spell of Manifest Destiny, and Texas (and the lands even farther west, still controlled by Mexico) seemed ripe for the plucking. Particularly galling to Americans was the fact that these lands, so plentiful in resources and almost screaming for development, remained in the hands of an inferior race. An American visitor to the Mexico territory of California in the early 1840s could barely contain his frustration. Lazy, beholden to the Catholic Church, brutal, and ignorant, the Mexicans in California were unworthy to control such a valuable piece of property. They were "an imbecile, pusillanimous, race of men, and unfit to control the destinies of that beautiful country." Fortunately, he concluded, nature would take its course. The same racial law that "curses the mulatto here with a constitution less robust than that of either race from which he sprang, lays a similar penalty upon the mingling of the Indian and white races in California and Mexico. They must fade away."

James K. Polk could not have agreed more and made the annexation of the Texas and California territories keystones of his successful 1844 campaign for the presidency. Texas, absorbed through a congressional resolution in early 1845, was already in American hands by the time Polk took office. But America still coveted the other massive holdings of Mexico in the west. American newspapers and speeches in Washington and around the country were liberally sprinkled with the terms "destiny of the race," "the path of progress," and more often, the "march of civilization." For a people who had spent the last two hundred years clearing the land of red men and enslaving black men to work it, there was little hesitation in deciding that the "imbecile" Mexicans must also give way to the pressures of Anglo-Saxon expansion. After some desultory attempts at diplomacy to try and buy the desired territories from Mexico, Polk quickly resorted to direct means. He sent American troops to the Rio Grande, claiming it to be the true boundary between Mexico and the United States. Mexico disagreed and dispatched its own troops to the river. After several tense months the inevitable occurred: shots were fired and President Polk proclaimed that American blood had been shed on American soil. By mid-1846 the two nations were at war.

Americans could not contain themselves in expressing their pious justifications for the conflict or their disdain for the enemy they now faced. As one newspaper declared, "We must march from ocean to ocean. We must march from Texas straight to the Pacific ocean. It is the destiny

Editorial cartoon portraying Mexican "rulers" departing Matamoras after the town was taken by American troops in 1846. The cartoon manages to use many of the stereotypes connected to Latin Americans: the "rulers" are, in fact, Catholic clergy, their "treasures" are basically comprised of alcohol and young women, and, as befitted what most Americans of the time considered a "mongrel" race, they flee at the first sign of danger. Source: "The Mexican Rulers, Migrating From Matamoras With Their Treasures," probable artist Frances Palmer (Lith. & pub. by F. & S. Palmer, 43 Ann St., New York), c. 1846, Library of Congress Prints and Photographs Division, LC-USZ62-35464.

of the white race, it is the destiny of the Anglo-Saxon Race." Another optimistically opined that America could "regenerate and disenthrall the people of Mexico" and that it was the nation's "destiny to civilize that beautiful country." The *American Review* was less certain, claiming that Mexico would soon find itself "yielding to a superior population, insensibly oozing into her territories, changing her customs, and out-living, exterminating her weaker blood."[5] By 1848 the war was over, with Mexico thoroughly defeated and American troops in control of Mexico City. Mexico was stripped of nearly two-thirds of its territory. The very ease of the conquest merely supported many Americans' belief that the Mexicans were inferior humans, not worthy of the bountiful lands they once had and unable to stand against the crushing tide of Anglo-Saxon progress and civilization.

Ironically, race served to forestall the annexation of all of Mexico after the conflict. With the Mexican nation prostrate before the Americans, the idea of simply taking the entire nation was initially attractive to some in the United States. Soon, however, other Americans vigorously attacked the idea. Some were guided by a fear that the additional territory would become, as Texas already had, part of the slave-holding South. The issue that seemed to seal the debate was one of the same issues that led the United States to proceed to take Mexico's land in the first place: race. It was one thing to argue that the United States was "destined" to take Texas, the vast New Mexico territory, and even California because the inferior Mexicans were unable to develop the lands for themselves. Those territories were sparsely populated. The assumption was that the Mexican populations in those lands would simply "fade away" as the Native Americans had. The southern portions of Mexico were quite a different matter. There, millions of Mexicans lived. Critics of the "all Mexico" position pointed out the futility (and possible danger) of U.S. annexation of an area populated by so many "mongrels." Surely, they cried, no one was suggesting that these people could ever be successfully assimilated into Anglo-Saxon America? As Representative Jacob Collamer proclaimed during the debate on the annexation of Mexico, "we should destroy our own nationality by such an act. We shall cease to be the people that we were; we cease to be the Saxon Americanized." Another congressman asked his colleagues whether they truly believed that America could, "by an act of Congress, convert the black, white, red, mongrel, miserable population of Mexico—the Mexicans, Indians, Mulattoes, Mestizos, Chinos, Zambos, Quinteros—into free and enlightened American citizens?"[6] The United States had taken what it wanted, and so what remained of the Mexican nation was left to its own devices to try and build a future.

II

Manifest Destiny resulted in the annexation of nearly one-half of the present-day United States. But it did not seem to bring peace and happiness to the restless Anglo-Saxon race. Just a few years following the war with Mexico, Americans engaged in a bloody civil war, achieving what would have been unimaginable at the hands of a foreign enemy: the slaughter of more than six hundred thousand of their own people. With the war over, old patterns reemerged rapidly. The idea that America's fortune and progress (and that of the Anglo-Saxon race) lay westward had not disappeared. In the decades after the Civil War the United States again looked beyond its borders, this time seeking markets and resources rather than land. And once again, the American gaze fell upon lands and peoples quite strange and, in most cases, virtually unknown to most U.S. citizens.

In short order, American racial views ordered these people—at once alluring and repugnant, enticing and dangerous—into familiar hierarchies of superiority and inferiority, serving as both a motivation and justification for the imperial thrust of the United States in the late nineteenth century.

America's overseas expansion of the late 1800s, climaxing in the Spanish-American War of 1898, was motivated by a number of factors. Certainly, economics played a major role. Disastrous depressions in the 1870s, 1880s, and again in the 1890s led some American businessmen and politicians to postulate that the cause of the "boom-bust" U.S. economy lay in the overproduction of agricultural and industrial goods. Markets became glutted, demand slackened, and prices fell. Farmers went even further into debt and factory workers often found themselves unemployed. As Senator Albert J. Beveridge argued in 1898, "Today we are raising more than we can consume. Today we are making more than we can use. . . . Therefore we must find new markets for our produce, new occupation for our capital, new work for our labor." And as Beveridge and others of his time well knew, economic problems quickly translated into social and political problems. Massive labor strikes wracked the nation in the last quarter of the nineteenth century, and farmers took things a step further by serving as one of the guiding forces behind the establishment of a new political party, the People's Party (more commonly known as the Populists). New markets overseas—particularly the "great China market," where hundreds of millions of Chinese were thought to eagerly await America's overproduction—were trumpeted as the solution to everyone's problems.

But other forces were at work as well. Military strategists, most notably Capt. Alfred Thayer Mahan, argued that a large navy was the key to power in the modern world. In two massive studies published in 1890 and 1892, Mahan traced the influence of sea power on world history. His conclusion was simple and direct: the nation that controlled the oceans controlled trade, power, and wealth. If it wished to join the ranks of the truly great powers and protect itself from predatory enemies, the United States had to increase its navy and take the overseas bases and coaling stations necessary to serve its ships. Religion also entered the picture. Facing what some Americans believed to be a moral crisis in the late nineteenth century (declining church attendance and a near-worship of science were cited as evidence), churches and congregations decided that it was time for action. Part of the call to arms involved a heavy emphasis on missionary work, for how could anyone truly claim to be a Christian if they left the heathens of the world to their fate? Thus began what some historians have referred to as "muscular Christianity," an emphasis on the need for strong souls *and* strong bodies to brave the wilds of Asia, Africa, and elsewhere to spread the word of God. Other historians have suggested that even issues of gender were involved. With individuals such as Theodore Roosevelt extolling the "rugged life" and complaining about the "overcivilization" that threatened the masculinity of the American male in the increasingly urbanized and mechanized world of the late 1800s, Americans sought avenues for regaining that lost vigor and virility. Sports saw a rapid rise in their popularity. And soon some theorists suggested that while sports provided one kind of field of battle on which a man could test himself, nothing could substitute for the real thing. Our forefathers hardened themselves in battle—the American Revolution, the War of 1812, the Mexican War, the Civil War. Perhaps a new test was needed.

It is unlikely that any one of these factors, taken individually, would have been sufficient to shape and mold America's imperialist expansion of the 1890s into the form it finally took. One element, however, ran like a thread through them, linking them into an imperial outlook that viewed much of the rest of the world as a tempting target for American expansion and military and economic domination. That element was race, and it soon served to both motivate American expansion into and justify its domination of two targets: Cuba and the Philippines.

By the late nineteenth century the debate over race had been reinvigorated, refocused, and sharpened. To a large degree, the instigator of this renewed discussion was Charles Darwin. His monumental 1859 study, *The Origin of Species*, effectively answered (though it did not silence) those who believed that one great creator brought the world and all its creatures into being at one time. Darwin's theories of evolution, though they were not entirely new and groundbreaking, were the first real attempt to systematically and scientifically explain the great differences between species and the changes in those species that took place over time. His idea of natural selection—the idea that nature "selected" different traits of a certain species to survive while others withered away—was a direct assault on much of the accepted theology of his day. Nevertheless, despite the controversies it engendered, the book soon set the standard against which other natural histories were measured.

Darwin limited his 1859 study to animals and flowers, but it raised one obvious question: Where does man fit in all of this? The theorist addressed the issue in his 1871 book, *The Descent of Man*. While it did not attract the readership of his 1859 study, *Descent of Man* certainly managed to create its own wealth of controversy. The apparent brutality of Darwin's conclusions stunned his readers. He suggested that in the "savage" world, those "weak in body or mind are soon eliminated." Darwin contrasted the savages with "civilized men" who did their "utmost to check the process of elimination" through asylums, hospitals, and care for the "imbecile, the maimed, and the sick." The result was that the "weak members of civilized societies propagate their kind." Those who raised domestic animals, he continued, recognized the hard fact that the weaklings must be culled from the herd. Yet, "excepting in the case of man himself, hardly anyone is so ignorant as to allow his worst animals to breed." Critics claimed that Darwin was calling for a crusade against the "weak" and "maimed," a wholesale slaughter of the "worst animals." A more careful reading of the book, however, suggests that while Darwin the scientist could objectively argue that the elimination of the weak improved the overall quality of the rest of a "herd," Darwin the human noted that his species exhibited sympathy toward such unfortunates. "Nor," he declared, "could we check our sympathy, even at the urging of hard reason, without deterioration in the noblest part of our nature."

American readers would have been struck by Darwin's comments on the United States in *Descent of Man*. The nation's "progress" and the "character of its people," he suggested, were the "results of natural selection." These "energetic, restless, and courageous men," invested with the bloodlines of the Anglo-Saxon, were leading their nation to a future of infinite wealth and power. Darwin cited with approval the words of one of his contemporaries who declared that, "All other series of events—as that which resulted in the culture of mind in Greece, and that which resulted in the empire of Rome—only appear to have purpose and value when viewed in connection with, or rather as subsidiary to . . . the great stream of Anglo-Saxon emigration to the west." It was no less than Americans themselves had always believed, but now it had the support of the most famous scientist in the world.

While Darwin was certainly known and read in the United States, a variant of his theory came to dominate the discussions in America among learned men, politicians, and the public at large concerning race, expansion, and imperialism. This variant was known as social Darwinism. Darwin's fellow Englishman, Herbert Spencer, is generally spotlighted as the foremost proponent of social Darwinism. Present-day historians and scientists, however, disagree as to whether what came to be popularly known in the United States as social Darwinism was really an accurate depiction of Spencer's wide-ranging and often convoluted theories. What does seem very clear is that a variety of intellectuals, scholars, politicians, and even religious figures in America claimed to find deep meaning in Spencer's writings, speeches, and lectures. (Spencer visited the United States in the early 1880s and addressed audiences that included industrialist Andrew Carnegie and former secretary of state William Evarts.)

What seemed to appeal most to Spencer's American readers and listeners was one particular phrase: "survival of the fittest." Usually associated with Darwin, in fact Spencer coined the term, as well as the phrase "struggle for existence." In an America where the gap between the rich and poor was growing dramatically, where some men accumulated massive fortunes while others eked out livings on the fringes of society, and where dramatic changes wrought by industrialization and urbanization had taken place in the space of a few short decades, the idea that Darwin's theories of natural evolution could be applied with equal success to human society were appealing to men like Carnegie. The steel baron once commented that after reading Spencer, "light came in as a flood and all was clear." And thus was born social Darwinism, a theory that suggested that just as in the jungle, competition for survival took place in the society of men and women. As with animals and flowers, those best suited to the changing environment (political, economic, cultural) would thrive and prosper. Those less able to cope would fade away. All of this, of course, was for the best, since the withering away of the weaker elements of a society would rebound to the benefit of that society as a whole. And thus light flooded in for Andrew Carnegie and others who came to endorse the philosophy of social Darwinism. The fact that some people seemed to struggle for existence was not the fault of any human agency. It was merely the working out of the laws of natural selection, and who could argue with nature?

It did not take much stretching of the theory of social Darwinism to bring race within its purview. If, as the theory suggested, there were stronger and weaker individuals within any given society, then it stood to reason that that there were stronger and weaker societies, nations, and races. William Graham Sumner, one of the most vigorous supporters of Spencer in the United States, who was sometimes referred to as the father of American sociology, claimed that one had to "draw the line somewhere" when debating the idea of whether all men were truly created equal. To those who thought otherwise, Sumner would ask "whether he thought the Bushmen, Hottentots, or Australians were equal to the best educated and most cultivated white men. He would have to admit that he was not thinking of them at all."[7]

The most vociferous proponent of social Darwinism in the United States, however, was very definitely thinking about the Bushmen,

Hottentots, and Australians of the world. John Fiske began his professional career as a lawyer but found himself increasingly fascinated by Spencer's theories. In 1873 he published an article entitled "The Progress From Brute to Man." In it he extolled the evolutionist outlook but also made some pointed remarks concerning differences between races. He lauded the "refined and intellectual Teuton" with 114 cubic inches of brain (the fascination with measuring the capacity of craniums did not dissipate in the nineteenth century). He contrasted this with the chimpanzee's brain, which was about one-quarter the size of the Teuton's. In between these two, however, lay the "Australian" with a brain larger than the chimp, but much smaller than the Teuton. He concluded from his study that "The capability of progress . . . is by no means shared alike by all races of men. Of the numerous races historically known to us, it has been manifested in a marked degree only by two—the Aryan and Semitic. To a much less conspicuous extent it has been exhibited by the Chinese and Japanese, the Copts of Egypt, and a few of the highest American races. On the other hand, the small-brained races—the Australians and Papuans, the Hottentots, and the majority of the tribes constituting the wide-spread Malay and American families—appear almost wholly incapable of progress, even under the guidance of higher races."[8]

By the 1880s and 1890s Fiske turned his attention to the study of history, particularly U.S. history. He lectured widely to large audiences and published an enormous number of popular histories. In his lectures, books, and articles, Fiske pounded home the same message: that the tremendous progress of the "Anglo-Saxon race" was merely the working of natural selection. The fittest (Americans and the English were about the only people Fiske would allow into the inner circle) made tremendous strides. The British empire and America's conquest of most of the North American continent gave the English-speaking races control of more than one-third of the planet. And while at times Fiske declared that he was in no way calling for further military conquests by the Anglo-Saxons, the none too subtle underpinnings of his arguments were clear. Most other races were "almost wholly incapable of progress," while the Anglo-Saxons brought development and civilization to every land they touched.

Fiske's audience must have also realized that it had been some time since American Anglo-Saxons spread their civilization and progress. Anglo-Saxon lore always accentuated the restless, expansive nature of the people. Whenever stagnation or social or political problems seemed to threaten the development of the race, the answer had always lay to the west—first Great Britain, then America—for rejuvenation, reinvigoration, reinvention. In the tumultuous years of the late nineteenth century, more than one American mulled these ideas over and began to wonder whether the march to the Pacific Coast would bring Anglo-Saxon progress to a standstill. That was what historian Frederick Jackson Turner seemed to suggest when he presented his essay, "The Significance of the Frontier in American History," at the 1893 World's Columbian Exposition in Chicago. Turner began by noting that the census of 1890 declared that there was no longer a discernible and definable American "frontier" line in the west. Turner pondered what this meant for America. In his opinion, the character, institutions, and qualities of the American people and nation were largely a result of a constant movement westward. Each surge into the wild frontier "did indeed furnish a new field of opportunity, a gate of escape from the bondage of the past." Reaching further into the past, Turner suggested, "What the Mediterranean Sea was to the Greeks, breaking the bond of custom, offering new experiences, calling out new institutions and activities, that, and more, the ever retreating frontier has been to the United States." By the 1890s, however, that frontier was gone, "and with its going has closed the first period of American history." Turner was quick to point out that it would be a "rash prophet who should assert that the expansive character of American life has now entirely ceased." For some Americans, Turner's message was clear. The frontier had been essential in forging the unique character and institutions of the Anglo-Saxons (as it always had been in Anglo-Saxon mythology). With the passing of America's continental frontier, new frontiers were needed.

The logical new frontier lay overseas; this was hardly an original thought in the latter part of the nineteenth century. Between the 1870s and 1900 Britain colonized more than four million square miles; France claimed over three million; Germany and Belgium each conquered another million square miles. Neither social Darwinism nor Turner's frontier thesis would have been sufficient in and of itself to propel America into joining the imperialistic frenzy that engulfed massive parts of Africa, Asia, and the Middle East in the late 1800s. As noted earlier, other forces—economic, religious, military/strategic, and even social/cultural—were at work pushing the United States to enter the race for overseas empire. Nevertheless, both social Darwinism and Turner's theory provided a solid racial basis upon which these other factors settled quite comfortably.

Reverend Josiah Strong, for example, had little difficulty equating the spread of Christianity with the spread of the Anglo-Saxon race. He laid out his thinking, a blend of missionary fervor, Darwinism, and imperialism, in his 1885 publication, *Our Country*. The book sold tens of thousands of copies. For Strong, the history of mankind was that of one race supplanting another. This had gone on for centuries, and more recently "the aborigines of North America, Australia and New Zealand are now disappearing before the all-conquering Anglo-Saxons. It would seem as if these inferior tribes were only precursors of a superior race, voices in the wilderness crying 'Prepare ye the way of the Lord!'" It was time, he declared, for the American Anglo-Saxon Christians to expand even farther. "If I read not amiss, this powerful race will move down upon Mexico, down upon Central and South America, out upon the islands of the sea, over upon Africa and beyond. And can any one doubt that the results of this competition of races will be the 'survival of the fittest?'" Not even the threat of enervating tropical climates could dampen Strong's enthusiasm. "The Anglo-Saxon has established himself in climates totally diverse—Canada, South Africa, and India—and, through several generations, has preserved his essential race characteristics. He is not, of course, superior to climatic influences; but even in warm climates, he is likely to retain his aggressive vigor long enough to supplant races already enfeebled. . . . Thus, while on this continent God is training the Anglo-Saxon race for its mission, a complemental work has been in progress in the great world beyond. God has two hands. Not only is he preparing in our civilization the die with which to stamp the nations, but, by what Southey called the 'timing of Providence,' he is preparing mankind to receive our impress."[9] God, it seemed, did indeed work in mysterious ways.

Men of the sword, as well as men of the cloth, found race a useful tool in buttressing their arguments about the need for a strong U.S. military, particularly a powerful navy. Rear Adm. Stephen B. Luce wrote in 1891, "War is one of the great agencies by which human progress is effected." Injecting a bit of Darwin and Spencer into his argument, Luce argued, "strife in one form or another in the organic world seems to be the law of existence." As for Mahan, in his public writings he talked in general terms about how "struggle" and "conflict" were the keystones of human existence and argued that a strong navy would provide the best defense for the United States. He was also clear about colonization. "Colonies attached to the mother-country afford, therefore, the surest means of supporting abroad the sea power of a country." Privately, Mahan confided that part of human conflict involved the racial struggle. He called for a closer working relationship between the two great Anglo-Saxon powers, the United States and Great Britain, in extending the power of the race to others in "the childhood stage of race development." Disparaging remarks about Latin Americans, Asians, and Africans merely supported his contention that the Anglo-Saxon provided "the best hope of the world."[10]

Race also crept into discussions about masculinity, virility, and imperialism. Theodore Roosevelt, who urged the "strenuous life" for all of his fellow Americans, was particularly concerned about what he perceived as a distinct loss of manliness in late-nineteenth-century America and what this might portend in the "struggle for survival." As historian Thomas Dyer suggests, Roosevelt strongly believed that, "To avoid decadence and to predominate, a race had to maintain the manly virtues: it had to work well, fight well, and breed well." (That latter point became something of an obsession for Roosevelt, who later in life championed the cause of white women having as many children as possible in order to "out-produce" the lesser races.) Roosevelt expressed his concern that "there are grave signs of deterioration in the English-speaking peoples." This deterioration might eventually result in a people who would be "quite unable to hold its own in those conflicts through which alone any great race can ultimately march to victory." In the main, the conflicts Roosevelt spoke of in the late 1800s concerned American overseas expansion. Only hardy, virile, manly Americans could carry out the tough work of imperialism, particularly when faced with an array of savage, inferior races. Considering the acquisition of Hawaii as essential to the imperial mission, Roosevelt worried that if the islands were not taken "it will show that we either have lost, or else wholly lack, the masterful instinct which alone can make a race great."[11]

Even the economic argument for imperialism, which was seemingly powerful enough in and of itself, benefited from American views of race. Some Americans, such as Josiah Strong, saw the race for empire as nothing less than a race for the survival of the Anglo-Saxon. "The unoccupied arable lands of the earth are limited, and will soon be taken. The time is coming when the pressure of population on the means of subsistence will be felt here as it is now felt in Europe and Asia. Then will the world enter upon a new stage of history—*the final competition of races, for which the Anglo-Saxon is being schooled*" (Strong's italics).[12] Most people in the United States, however, would not go so far as to give credence to the Malthusian catastrophe that Strong described. A more convincing argument for most Americans was in the florid speeches of Albert Beveridge. Speaking shortly after the Spanish-American War, the senator made clear that the wealth of the Far East was nearly unimaginable: "vegetable and mineral riches," "mountains of coal," and nuggets of gold. For Beveridge the issue was not that resources were in short supply and the United

States had to take what it could. Instead, like many Americans, he could but shake his head when he considered the lack of development in these regions. China was a perfect example. "Her resources, her possibilities, her wants, all are undeveloped." He witnessed the same thing in the Philippines, now under the control of the United States. There was unbelievably rich land and deposits of minerals that boggled the mind. As evidence of this wealth he displayed a gold nugget and gold dust from the islands. Yet, the dust had been "washed out by crude processes of careless natives." It was little wonder to Beveridge that the Philippines remained poor and undeveloped. The Filipinos themselves were a "barbarous race, modified by three centuries of contact with a decadent race [the Spanish]." Quite simply, people such as these were incapable of harnessing—or perhaps even understanding—the great wealth they possessed. They were people of "superstition," "dishonesty," and "disorder in habits of industry." When some American expressed concern that cheap Filipino labor might flood the United States, the senator was incredulous. "Whips of scorpions could not lash the Filipinos to this land of fervid enterprise, sleepless industry, and rigid order." His message was clear enough. It was necessary for the brawny, intelligent, orderly Anglo-Saxons to step in and bring efficiency to such lands (and, subsequently, profit to the United States).[13]

The Spanish-American War, which began in April 1898, demonstrated the amazing adaptability of American racism and its usefulness for empire building. The war with Spain and the acquisition of Cuba and the Philippines (among other territories) as a result of that conflict were jarring events for Americans. While many could agree with the chest-thumping Anglo-Saxonism of the late 1800s, the need for overseas markets, or even the necessity of "saving" the heathen souls of those abroad, it soon became evident that imperialism was not as simple or clear-cut as it seemed. Certainly, expansion was nothing new to American history, but the expansion of the 1890s was something different. In America's Anglo-Saxon lore, previous movements west and south had been into "uninhabited" lands—a few Native Americans or Mexicans to be brushed aside, but basically "virgin territory" into which flowed thousands of sturdy whites. This would not be the case with Cuba and the Philippines. Both were heavily populated by non-white people. It was obvious to most Americans that these new lands, with few exceptions, would not be populated by eager Anglo-Saxons who would eventually push aside the natives. Some journalists and congressmen could still trumpet America's "manifest destiny," but the outward thrust of the 1890s was not the same.

This would be imperialism: wars would be fought; lands would be conquered; native peoples would be subdued; and the United States would become a colonial power. How could liberty-loving Anglo-Saxons, who had themselves fought to free their land from the evils of despotic colonial rule, create an empire?

Perhaps that perplexing question was one reason the conflict with Spain was originally portrayed as one that would free Cubans from the evil clutches of their colonial masters. In this regard, familiar racial stereotypes served a useful purpose. At least initially, American newspapers and many politicians painted the rebellious Cuban people as desperate victims of Spanish cruelty and abuse. This fit in quite well with the old Black Legend, and the American audience eagerly awaited each new tale of Spanish calumny and villainy. It was not disappointed. Newspaper articles and editorial cartoons depicted the Spanish officials and soldiers as dark, seedy, and disreputable characters who thought nothing of killing children or torturing and raping women. The Cuban people usually found themselves cast in the role of a helpless and weak female, waiting for her chivalrous knight (the United States) to save her. Again, this rang true with the American audience that had always believed Latin Americans to be effeminate. As historian John J. Johnson notes, however, these portrayals of the Cubans differed in some ways from the old, harsher depictions of Latin Americans.[14] The Cuban women in the editorial cartoons that filled American newspapers were usually strikingly beautiful, almost enticing. They were also noticeably whiter than the usual pictures of Latin Americans. Newspaper and magazine stories accentuated the high percentage of European blood and the relative paucity of black blood on the island. Some pundits even referred to the Cubans as "bronzed Europeans." Thus, William McKinley, in his war message to Congress in April 1898 could cite as one of the chief reasons for the American intervention in Cuba the "cause of humanity." A little over a week after McKinley's speech Congress passed the Teller Amendment in which the United States dismissed any intention of taking control of Cuba—"except for the pacification thereof."

Yet, once American troops, officials, and reporters flooded into Cuba following the "splendid little war," U.S. attitudes quickly hardened toward the "bronzed Europeans" they had just "liberated." Americans were aghast to discover not heavily suntanned Europeans, but the same mixed, "mongrel" race that they believed characteristic of every Latin American nation. Most important, they found that a large number of the brave Cuban rebels were, in fact, black. The change in the portrayal of the Cubans in the American media was immediate. Gone were the raven-haired damsels of the prewar period. A new stereotype now came to the fore. In truth, it was a very old stereotype, modified for the Cuban experience: the typical Cuban was portrayed as an African American. The same huge lips, wild hair, and enormous, vague eyes used to denote the recently freed black Americans in cartoons, drawings, and paintings were transplanted to depictions of Cubans. Almost invariably, the new Cubans, like blacks, were portrayed as children—sometimes ignorant, sometimes throwing temper tantrums, sometimes engaging in unspeakable cruelty, but always in need of constant supervision and discipline. Certain modifications needed to be made, of course. In place of the straight razor (which was thought to be the preferred weapon of the African American) came the machete. Sombreros replaced straw hats because it was assumed that all Latin Americans wore sombreros. And just so the white American audience would not get too confused, the name "Cuba" was emblazoned across the caricatures' shirts or hats. In many of the cartoons, a patient, tolerant, but firm Uncle Sam who was doing his best to keep the unruly Cuban child under control represented the United States. The message was effective. White Americans from both the North and South had come to agree by the 1890s that African Americans were too inferior and reckless to have any voice in the U.S. government. By transplanting the African-American stereotype to Cuba, American public opinion makers were suggesting that it was even more unreasonable to assume that the lazy, ignorant, vicious, backward Cubans could take upon themselves the mantle of self-government. The "pacification" of Cuba, therefore, ended up taking quite a bit longer than first imagined, and the Platt Amendment of 1903 gave the United States virtually complete control of the island.[15]

Filipinos were not quite as fortunate. In the months leading up to the Spanish-American War the fate of the Philippines was not a main point of public discussion. In fact, many Americans seemed somewhat surprised to learn that their nation had seized the islands from the Spanish—and intended to stay. President McKinley admitted that when "the Philippines had dropped into our laps I confess I did not know what to do with them." Eventually, however, he sought the highest counsel available—God—who answered his fervent prayer, telling the president that "there was nothing left for us to do but to take them all, and to educate the Filipinos, and uplift and civilize and Christianize them." He then "went to bed, and went to sleep, and slept soundly."[16] Although the Filipinos had engaged in ongoing rebellion against Spanish rule, they never became "bronzed Europeans." Almost immediately, the Filipinos were portrayed in the popular press and in speeches as tribal people, completely given over to savagery. As Beveridge asked, "shall we leave them to themselves? Shall tribal wars scourge them, disease waste them, savagery brutalize them more and more? Shall their fields lie fallow, their forests rot, their mines remain sealed, and all the purposes and possibilities of nature be nullified?"[17] When the Filipino rebels had the audacity to turn their fire on the Americans, Roosevelt was livid, calling the leader of the Filipino resistance "the typical representative of savagery, the typical foe of civilization and the American people."[18] In editorial cartoons, the Filipinos got roughly the same treatment as Cubans in one regard: cartoonists used African-American stereotypes to portray them as childlike and in need of discipline. Americans in the Philippines routinely referred to the natives

Editorial cartoon from 1898 showing President William McKinley with members of his new "family" of conquered lands: Cuba, the Philippines, and Puerto Rico. Note that each of the figures representing these very different peoples and cultures are drawn using the stereotypical fashion usually reserved for illustrations of African Americans—another suggestion to the white American reading public that the United States was dealing with decidedly inferior peoples in these overseas possessions. In addition, the "soapbox" upon which McKinley sits is not without meaning. It was a "prop" often used in such cartoons to suggest that what the "natives" needed was a good "washing" at the hands of their new white masters. Source: J. Campbell Cory, "The Cares of a Growing Family," The Bee, May 25, 1898, General Research Division, The New York Public Library, Astor, Lenox, and Tilden Foundations.

as "niggers." This image of Filipinos was gradually modified, however, as the Filipino Insurrection (1899–1902) began to require more American troops and to result in more American deaths. Having easily transposed their views of African Americans onto the inhabitants of the Philippines, Americans took what was a logical step: they called on even older racial stereotypes of the Native Americans. The backward and primitive, yet stealthy and deadly Indian seemed a more appropriate template on which to redraw the Filipino. In just a short period, newspapers were describing the Filipino "braves" and comparing them to Apaches or Comanches.

U.S. forces subjected Filipinos, as savages, to brutal treatment with little hesitation. Testimony of American soldiers indicated a long list of tortures inflicted on prisoners: brandings, beatings, shootings, strangling, and the infamous "water torture," in which water was forced down a man's throat until he could not breath, or until his stomach became bloated with the fluid after which he would be punched and kicked until he talked or an internal organ burst. Whether portrayed as black or red, the Filipinos were reduced to targets. As one soldier wrote home about the "nigger fighting business" in the Philippines, "I am in my glory when I can sight my gun on some dark skin and pull the trigger."[19] When the insurrection was finally put down, more than four thousand Americans were dead. Estimates of Filipino deaths ranged into the hundreds of thousands, brought on by both the fighting and starvation as their lands and homes were systematically destroyed.

The cost, in money and blood, of the war in the Philippines began to call into question America's imperial destiny. A small but vocal group of Americans, who came to be known as the "anti-imperialists" raised serious doubts about whether America should even be in the Philippines. Part of their rhetoric was cloaked in the language of democracy and freedom for all people. But the most powerful argument in their arsenal was the race problem. Turning the imperialists' arguments back against them, they asked, if the Filipinos were such savages, completely incapable of self-government and utterly immune to any hint of civilization, then what on earth was the United States doing in trying to colonize them? The answer from the imperialists demonstrated just how adaptable the race issue could be in serving the American imperial mission.

To fully comprehend the racial argument for the colonization of the Philippines, we must visit the city of St. Louis in the year 1904. Historian Robert Rydell, in his fascinating study of world's fairs held in America, takes us beyond the hoopla and sideshows and gimmicks at the Louisiana Purchase Exposition of 1904 to suggest ways in which the American exhibitions at the fair clearly—and scientifically—explained the rationale for America's role in the Philippines. It all began with the "Congress of Races," a massive anthropological display organized by some of the leading natural scientists in the United States. As one of them explained, the goal of the exhibit was simple and direct: "to represent human progress from the dark prime to the highest enlightenment, from savagery to civic organization, from egoism to altruism." Visitors were treated to a virtual tour of the history of mankind, from its days living in caves (savagery), to a somewhat better organized but still brutal society (barbarism), and then the long road from barbarism to civilization. Along the way, various races were displayed as examples of the stages of human development: skulls (always skulls), primitive wares and weapons, and so forth. At the end, the viewer came face to face with the epitome of racial and human progress: the Anglo-Saxon.

But what of the non-Anglo-Saxon people of the earth? Were they to be forever condemned to savagery and barbarism? The answers to these questions were found in what turned out to be the single most popular exhibit at the fair: the Philippine Reservation. Over twelve hundred Filipinos were brought to St. Louis and set up in their "natural habitats" for onlookers to gawk at. Beyond the revulsion and/or titillation of seeing "half-naked" savages (including one Filipino who was dubbed the "missing link" in the evolutionary scale of mankind), the tasteless human exhibition carried a message. The reservation was carefully constructed so that visitors were first introduced to the most "savage" and "primitive" of the Filipinos, situated in their quaint, but squalid, villages. From there, fairgoers entered the entirely different world of the "civilized" Filipino "tribes" that had benefited so very much from the American presence. No naked savages here; instead, the tourists saw Filipinos wearing Western dress, Filipino children attending school (and singing "My Country 'Tis of Thee"), and Filipino men and women dutifully at work at sewing machines and on other worthy tasks. As Rydell suggests, the meaning was clear to even the most casual observer. The "savage" Filipinos were the kind of people the Americans found when they landed in the islands in 1898. (An underlying theme was that this was how little the Filipinos had progressed during hundreds of years of Spanish rule.) The "civilized" Filipinos were the result of American efforts to instill Anglo-Saxon ways of life (if not, of course, Anglo-Saxon blood) into the inferior brown men and women. Thus, the Philippine Reservation provided a living laboratory for viewing the progress of mankind—and a forceful answer to the anti-imperialists. A kind of civilization was, therefore, possible in lands such as the Philippines—but *only* with constant U.S. supervision and tutelage. Remove the American presence, and the "missing links" would take over, reducing Filipino society to something approaching the Stone Age.

In 1899 the British writer Rudyard Kipling called on the white race to do its imperial duty overseas in his famous poem, "The White Man's Burden." In fact, however, the United States had taken on the burden years before under the rubric of Manifest Destiny. Crossing first a continent and then an ocean, the United States, in just a few years, brushed aside the Native Americans, the Mexicans, the Spanish, the Cubans, and the Filipinos to claim an empire that now spanned half the globe. Whether it was phrased as Manifest Destiny or the white man's burden, for Americans the central message had always been relatively clear and uncomplicated. The Anglo-Saxon race was destined to build a great empire, even if that meant the annihilation, displacement, or colonization of large numbers of inferior races. And at the end of the nineteenth century the United States stood astride its empire, the power of the Anglo-Saxon virtually unchallenged. As it turned out, the greatest challenge would come not from America's fellow Anglo-Saxons of Great Britain or its Teuton forefathers in Germany or even the brooding Slavic race of Russia. A new and powerful color was rising.

CHAPTER 3

YELLOW

I N **1913** THE READING PUBLIC IN Great Britain and the United States
was introduced to a new character. Arthur Ward, writing under the
pseudonym of Sax Rohmer, published the first of thirteen novels
featuring the classic villain, Dr. Fu-Manchu. *The Insidious Dr. Fu-Manchu*
(the title in England was *The Mystery of Dr. Fu-Manchu*) sold thousands of
copies in the United States, and the series remained popular right up to
the last book published in 1959, the year of Rohmer's death. It was not
long before Fu-Manchu made the transition to the silver screen. Portrayed by a number of actors over the years, the "evil genius" was featured in numerous films.

The first Fu-Manchu novel set the general tone for the series:
breathtaking chases, mysterious Oriental rituals, fantastic creatures, exotic and deadly poisons, damsels in distress, and last-minute heroics by
the stoic Englishman Denis Nayland Smith. As in so many novels and
movies concerning truly evil villains, Dr. Fu-Manchu was undoubtedly
the most interesting and intriguing character of all. In the early stages of
the book, Smith grimly describes his arch-nemesis:

> Imagine a person, tall, lean and feline, high-shouldered, with a
> brow like Shakespeare and a face like Satan, a close-shaven
> skull, and long, magnetic eyes of the true cat-green. Invest
> him with all the cruel cunning of an entire Eastern race, accu-
> mulated in one giant intellect, with all the resources, if you
> will, of a wealthy government—which, however, already has
> denied all knowledge of his existence. Imagine that awful be-
> ing, and you have a mental picture of Dr. Fu-Manchu, the
> yellow peril incarnate in one man.[1]

51

The American audience welcomed the appearance of Rohmer's novel and eagerly awaited and read the succeeding tales of adventure and intrigue. Partly, the allure of the books lay in their ability to take the American reader to new and exotic locales. They always included a host of fascinating characters from foreign lands. And Americans could take comfort in the fact that the villain was continually thwarted by his dogged, resourceful, and fantastically heroic Anglo-Saxon opponent. As for Fu-Manchu himself, he was in some ways a new and terrifying character. In fact, it can be argued that Fu-Manchu represented one of the first manifestations of a popular mainstay of later fiction and film: the evil "supergenius" intent on conquering the world. Yet, most Americans reading Rohmer's description of the Asian troublemaker were untroubled by the brutal racist stereotypes used to describe Fu-Manchu (and all other Asians) in the books. Long before the first novel hit the United States, Americans had been well aware of the yellow hordes of Asia—and the peril they posed to white society.

For the last part of the eighteenth century and the first half of the nineteenth century, most Americans had little knowledge of or interest in Asia. Only a handful of individuals from the United States experienced direct contact with the people of Asia, mostly the Chinese. These included a very small number of American missionaries endeavoring to save the heathens and a larger number of American traders endeavoring to profit from the heathens. As historian Stuart Miller makes clear in his thorough study of U.S. images of China during these early years, the American perception of the Chinese people was largely negative.[2] The Chinese were deceitful, and fraud and bribery were their preferred methods of conducting business. Many Americans simply found the Chinese "contemptible," and their government appeared to be despotic and often barbaric. Americans also sensed an innate backwardness in China, similar to the backwardness they saw in Latin America. Though the nation seemed to have riches aplenty—spices, silk, silver, gems, and opium—this great wealth had no discernible impact on China, which was often described as a nation static and stuck in time. The people were superstitious and a cloak of mysticism seemed to have enveloped them like a fog, always obscuring their true intentions and feelings from Anglo-Saxon visitors. That the British so handily defeated the Chinese in the Opium War of 1839–42 only cemented the impression that the "celestial kingdom" was a third-rate nation, at best. It was only a short step to considering that the primary source of China's weakness lay in its own people.

Miller suggests that blatantly racist opinions of the Chinese were rarely voiced in these first contacts. That may very well have been the case; after all, American racist views were just becoming hardened in the early nineteenth century and the Chinese—unlike Native Americans, Africans, and Latin Americans—did not suffer from proximity to the Anglo-Saxons. In addition, the traders and missionaries who found their way to China were there to conduct business, whether with the Bible or the account book. They had little time for scientific theorizing about the racial position of the Chinese. Nevertheless, as even Miller concludes, racism sometimes peeked through in the correspondence and diaries of American travelers to China. As one Yankee trader complained, the Chinese were "grossly superstitious . . . most depraved and vicious." He went on at length about their genius in the art of torture that could "only be conceived by a people refined in cruelty, blood thirsty and inhuman."[3] Indeed, it would have been surprising if these early American visitors did not harbor at least some racial ideas concerning the Asian peoples they met. From the very beginning of discussions about racial differences, Asians played a significant role. Carl Linnaeus created the category "Asiaticus" and opined that they were a money-grubbing, shallow people. Johann Friedrich Blumenbach was more specific, lumping the Chinese into a new heading, "Mongolian." And no race could escape the skull-clutching mania of Dr. Samuel George Morton, who concluded with his usual pinpoint scientific studies that Chinese skulls were barely eighty cubic inches in capacity—just above those of Native Americans and Africans. (Unfortunately for science, Morton was never able to accumulate enough Asian skulls for a complete study and so he was not able to produce a *Crania Asiatica* for the reading public.) Morton's avid disciple, Josiah Nott, also placed the Chinese somewhere in the middle of the pack in his own racial rankings.

The relative lack of interest in the Chinese people ended, however, with the California gold rush of 1849. Soon, thousands of Chinese poured into California to search for the precious metal. As Native Americans, Latin Americans, and Africans discovered before them, the Chinese immigrants quickly found that greater contact with Americans did not result in greater understanding or appreciation of cultural diversity. By the 1850s and 1860s most Americans viewed the immigrant Chinese, nearly 90 percent of whom were male, as merely an interesting source of cheap labor. The railroads were eager for people who would do the extraordinarily difficult and dangerous work associated with constructing the rail lines. And in a bizarre twist, in the years after the Civil War some plantation owners in the South tossed around the notion of importing Chinese labor to take the place of the recently freed slaves. In 1868 the United States and China signed the Burlingame Treaty, which stated that both nations would recognize the right of free and unrestricted immigration of the other's citizens into their respective nations. In addition, the United States promised that the Chinese coming to America would be granted the same privileges and rights as those given to immigrants from even the most favored nations. When it became obvious, however, that the new arrivals were not content to do the most menial labor and that some of them intended to stay, racial harassment began to grow, particularly on the American West Coast, where many of the Chinese congregated.

Soon, the Chinese were being portrayed as unwanted competitors for American jobs. Charges were leveled that the Chinese were, in fact, unfair competitors. Their perceived filthy habits, willingness (indeed, it appeared, eagerness) to live in squalor, and backward ways meant that they would work for wages far below those that any self-respecting white man would accept. Racial hatred superheated American criticisms of the Chinese immigrants. Politicians and others seeking power and prestige in California began to heap scorn upon the Chinese: they were generally found in opium dens (where they did their best to lure whites into using the drug); with few women of their own, the Chinese men preyed on white women, debasing them and often kidnapping them and selling them into prostitution. Terms such as "swarming masses" and "vermin" began to creep into discussions of the Chinese and—though there were only about one hundred thousand Chinese in the United States by 1880—a new and terrifying portrayal of the new immigrants began to emerge, one in which the "hordes" of yellow would sweep into and eventually overwhelm America's white population.

In short order, the United States reversed its position taken in the Burlingame Treaty and moved to both restrict Chinese immigration to America and make certain that the Chinese already in the country were deprived of any constitutional protections or rights of citizens. California took the lead, barring Chinese immigrants from testifying against whites in state courts in 1854. By 1870 the U.S. government became involved in the "Chinese question" and passed the Naturalization Act. By limiting American citizenship to "white persons and persons of African descent," the act effectively eliminated Asians from consideration. A Senate subcommittee, reacting to pleas from concerned whites in California, held hearings in 1876 to better determine the nature and extent of the Chinese threat to Anglo-Saxon America. A. A. Sargent (Republican-California) assumed leadership of the subcommittee and was primarily responsible for the language of the majority report, aptly described by historian Luther Spoehr as a "verbal blunderbuss." The Chinese lived in "filthy dwellings . . . disregarding health and fire ordinances." The willingness of the Chinese to accept wages that "would be starvation prices for white men and women" led to the fear that this situation would "degrade all white working people to the abject condition of a servile class." Any thoughts of assimilating the Chinese and granting them political and civil rights should be dismissed posthaste. "An indigestible mass in the community, distinct in language, pagan in religion, inferior in mental and moral qualities, and all peculiarities, is an undesirable element in a republic, but becomes especially so if political power is placed in its hands." Senator James G. Blaine, who became secretary of state in 1881, employed his usual florid style to declare, "Either the Anglo-Saxon race will possess the Pacific slope or the Mongolian will possess it." Writer P. W. Dooner added his own opinions to the growing anti-Chinese sentiment with his 1880 book, *Last Days of the Republic*. The novel recounted the horrible consequences of unlimited Chinese immigration: American democracy would soon be undermined and outnumbered whites would become slaves to their barbaric Asian masters.[4] The American government had heard enough, and in 1882 it passed the Chinese Exclusion Act, the first legislative act to single out a race of people as undesirable immigrants.

The act certainly made it more difficult for Chinese to enter the United States, but immigration did not entirely cease. Some immigrants claimed to be the relatives of Chinese already living in America; others simply slipped through the legal system and melted into the growing Chinese population in California. By the 1880s, however, "yellow peril" had achieved the status of accepted wisdom in the United States. It was an issue in the 1888 presidential race, during which President Grover Cleveland voiced his opinion that the immigrants were "dangerous to our peace and welfare." Samuel Gompers, head of the American Federation of Labor, feared that the Chinese and their Asian brethren would "overwhelm the world." The Chinese, in particular, had "no standard of morals by which a Caucasian may judge them." In 1901 Gompers produced a pamphlet entitled *Some Reasons for Chinese Exclusion; Meat vs. Rice: American Manhood Against Asiatic Coolieism—Which Shall Survive?* The main point of his treatise was that the Chinese were a particularly servile and submissive race. Unlike white Americans, the Chinese would not stand up for higher wages or better working conditions and thus threatened the rights of all American laborers.

The Chinese in America were one thing—an unpleasant, "indigestible," and perhaps threatening yellow mass. In China, however, they represented something quite different by the late nineteenth century. The

Cartoon showing presidential candidates James Garfield and Winfield Hancock nailing "John Chinaman" between their anti-Chinese party platforms. The drawing suggested the broad national agreement on the need to keep the Chinese out of America and also used the usual stereotypical form to illustrate the Chinese: traditional garb and hairstyle, a serpentlike tongue, and a devilish and frightening facial expression. Source: James A. Wales, "Where Both Platforms Agree— No Vote—No Use to Either Party," Puck, July 14, 1880, 335, Library of Congress Prints and Photographs Division, LC-USZC2-1232.

old perceptions of the Chinese as backward, corrupt, and greedy remained. What had changed, however, was America's need for Chinese consumers of its products. The last quarter of the nineteenth century saw the United States go through three horrible economic depressions, culminating with the collapse of 1893–97. One popular explanation for these unsettling events was the claim that American factories and farms were simply producing more than the U.S. market could consume, leading to frequent "gluts" and subsequent economic downturns. The solution seemed just as obvious: develop foreign markets to absorb the overproduction. With so much of the world already carved into imperial enclaves by the British, French, Dutch, Portuguese, Russians, and other powers, America soon set its sights on the millions and millions of potential customers in China. The perceived necessity for developing the "great China market" to relieve the surplus of overproduction in the United States in effect combined Americans' racist attitudes with the need to transform the Chinese into willing and eager consumers of American products. The Spanish-American War, which led to the seizure of the Philippines, and the annexation of other island chains in the Pacific, including Hawaii, brought Americans to the very doorstep of what was touted in newspapers and industry journals as a marvelously undeveloped market. Jealously guarding that door, however, were several nations that had a substantial jump on the United States. Great Britain, France, Portugal, the Netherlands, Germany, Russia, Japan, and other countries had already laid claim to their "spheres of influence" in China and were avidly carving up trade and investment opportunities. In response to this international presence, the United States issued the so-called Open Door Notes. These two diplomatic messages, sent in 1899 and 1900, implored the other powers to respect the right of all nations to equal access to China's trade and markets. Interestingly enough, only one power was left from the list of recipients: China itself.

The tenor of the Open Door Notes suggested the general U.S. attitude toward China and the Chinese people. Unable or unwilling to defend themselves against the predations of the imperial powers (the United States, of course, did not include itself under the rubric of "imperialist"), the Chinese necessarily needed the Americans' protection. The American press most often portrayed the Chinese as children—immature, undeveloped, emotional, sometimes given to violent outbursts and tantrums, but capable of at least remedial education. They could be Christianized and, of at least equal importance, they could be taught that the way to progress lay through the acceptance of a culture of consumption—enjoying the "finer things of life" that Americans nearly took for granted. This, unfortunately, was easier said than done. The Chinese seemed hopelessly backward and unfamiliar with (and even hostile to) the basic concepts of capitalism. As one American missionary complained, the Chinese were frugal to a fault and exhibited an "indifference to comfort and convenience." The missionary was astounded to find that Chinese clothing had no pockets and thus nowhere to put one's watch and other accoutrements of the civilized person. According to one of America's leading sociologists, to "westernize" China it would be incumbent upon the Chinese to make some revisions to their society: "dropping ancestor worship, dissolving the clan, educating girls, elevating women, postponing marriage, introducing compulsive education, restricting child labor and otherwise individualizing the members of the family."[5] With these few simple changes, China would be on the path to modernity.

When in 1900 the outbreak of the Boxer Rebellion seemed to suggest some reluctance on the part of the Chinese to accept wholesale alteration of their society, politics, and customs, American observers were frankly astounded. The rebellion, in which segments of Chinese society (many of them members of secret societies, popularly known as the Boxers) began to attack foreign missionaries and Chinese converts to Christianity, became so widespread that the foreign powers involved in the nation sent in thousands of troops to put it down. Eight nations, including the United States, contributed troops to the so-called International Relief Expedition, which eventually pushed the rebels back and relieved the virtual siege of various foreign embassies and consulates. The fighting was sometimes vicious and heavy. Thousands, and perhaps tens of thousands, of Chinese died during the conflict. The international forces suffered approximately 250 killed, including nearly thirty American marines killed and wounded. American astonishment at the violence in China was made up of mixed emotions. The first was a sense of betrayal. As John Hay, author of the Open Door Notes, later recalled, "We have done the Chinks a great service which they don't seem inclined to recognize."[6] Hay's puzzlement was genuine. The Chinese did not seem to understand or appreciate America's efforts (and those of some of the other Western powers) to bring civilization and progress to their backward society. Partially, too, the surprise was based on the very size and violence of the uprising. Here, on a limited scale, was the nightmare of the "yellow peril" played out in graphic detail: hordes of Chinese, seemingly indifferent to their own fate, throwing themselves against the bastions of Western civilization, culture, and power. They failed, but only because the military might of eight nations united to beat them back. In one way, however, the attacks were consistent with the American view of the Chinese. The Boxers targeted the weak and the unarmed, striking at diplomats and missionaries. The very fact that they killed missionaries and Chinese converts alike merely solidified the view that at the center of every "Chink" was a vicious heathen waiting to get out.

As frightening as the Chinese became in the American imagination, they were eventually pushed to the side by another, even more terrifying, Asian people. In early studies of differences between races, the Japanese were typically lumped in with the Chinese in the "Oriental" or "Asian" or "Mongolian" categories. And like the Chinese, the Japanese were of little interest to early nineteenth-century Americans. Even American traders saw little profit to be made in the strange island empire of Japan, until its "opening" by Como. Matthew Perry in 1853. If anything, Japan's self-imposed isolation up to the time of Perry's visit simply made it the most mysterious of the nations of the mysterious East. Wild tales abounded of the strange qualities of the Japanese and about the unfortunate shipwrecked sailors or misguided missionaries who happened to fall into their hands.

Once the United States and Japan began to make more consistent economic and political contacts, however, it became clear to many Americans that the Japanese were different. Not surprisingly, many of the same racially tinged observations that had been made about the Chinese were easily transposed to the Japanese. The famous writer and thinker Henry Adams set down his reflections on the Japanese people during a trip to their homeland in the 1880s. He found that the "natives, like all orientals, are children, and have the charms of childhood as well as the faults of the small boy." Overall, he declared the Japanese to be somewhat "primitive." Adams could not "conquer a feeling that the Japs are monkeys, and the women are very badly made monkeys."[7] Despite these ugly reminders that the Japanese were, after all, "Orientals," a number of Americans began to draw some distinctions between them and their Asian cousins, the Chinese. The Japanese seemed better organized (almost regimented) and more capable. Vivid evidence of this was the crushing Japanese defeat of China in the Sino-Japanese War of 1894–95. The ease with which the smaller nation dismantled the larger nation's army and navy suggested to a number of observers in the United States that Japan was at the top of the "Oriental" heap of humanity. When Japanese troops came to the assistance of the Western powers during the Boxer Rebellion, Theodore Roosevelt exclaimed (in a compliment, of sorts), "what extraordinary soldiers those little Japs are."

The Russo-Japanese War of 1904–1905 was both the highpoint of U.S. admiration of the competitive spirit and organizational abilities of the Japanese and the beginning of a more aggressive tone in American dealings with the upstart Asian power. In some ways, the American attitude toward Japan's military success against Russia was one of pride. Many

U.S. officials firmly believed that Japan's rise to the position of a world power began with its contact with America in the 1850s. Unlike the Chinese, who remained wedded to their backward and static social structures, the Japanese seemed to welcome Western influences in order to modernize their society and thereby make it more resistant to Western domination. More important, the Japanese possessed an uncanny ability to "mimic" or "ape" Western culture, technology, military tactics, and so forth. Thus developed one of the basic perceptions of the Japanese race: like children, they were able to "copy" what they saw in the Western powers, most notably the United States, and use this to their advantage. Roosevelt, who would later step in to mediate a peace between Japan and Russia, called the "Japs" a "wonderful people . . . quite as remarkable industrially as in warfare." They would soon, he announced, take their place as a "great civilized power of a formidable type."[8]

And therein lay the problem. The Japanese rise to power in the late nineteenth and early twentieth centuries was rapid and aggressive. They had already laid claim to rights and spheres of influence in China by way of their victory in the 1890s conflict. They acquired more territory and more influence with their showing against the massive Russian empire. As proud as America was of its Japanese "students," it was also deeply troubled by the ascension of the Land of the Rising Sun to a position of power in the Far East. For all of their "mimicry" of Western ways, the Japanese would never be accepted as equals. They might be at the apex of the "Oriental" racial variety of humanity, but that merely meant that they were the best of an inferior—and potentially dangerous—race. Simply put, the Japanese posed a threat to the carefully constructed theories on race that guided American thinking for centuries. The racial order upon which world power seemed to rest was under attack. The Japanese had already humbled one white power (albeit, as many U.S. officials observed, a "Slavic" white power) with their victories against Russia. Dr. Fu-Manchu might have been the most popular fictional representation of the "yellow peril," but even before Rohmer's first novel appeared in 1913, Americans already faced a very real example of that threat in the form of Japan.

Japan certainly posed a perplexing problem: a rising world power that was neither Anglo-Saxon nor even white. How was it to be treated? Here again, American racial perceptions came to play a key role. For example, despite Japan's military and political accomplishments, the American attitude toward Japanese immigrants to the United States was quite similar to that exhibited toward the Chinese. Again, the flashpoint for this antagonism was California, where thousands of Japanese settled during the 1880s, 1890s, and early 1900s. "The Japs must go!" was a familiar refrain among politicians, newspapers, and anti-immigrant groups in the state. Japan's rise to the status of a world power did nothing to assuage the fears and anger of whites; in fact, it only increased those feelings. As one newspaper editorialized, "Once the war with Russia is over, the brown stream of Japanese immigration [will become] a raging torrent." Calls went out for new legislation to complement the Chinese Exclusion Act and bar Japanese immigration. In 1906 the San Francisco school board announced the establishment of separate school facilities for Asian children.

This was a ticklish problem for the U.S. government. Roosevelt, who became president upon the assassination of William McKinley in 1901, admired some characteristics of the Japanese but was growing wary of their increasing clout in the Far East. To exclude the Chinese meant offending a virtually powerless and backward people who could not possibly retaliate in any meaningful way against the United States. Japan, however, was a force to be reckoned with and might not take such slights lying down. Roosevelt was adamant in his opposition to Japanese immigration. The pathways of development "of the Orient and the Occident, have been separate and divergent since thousands of years before the Christian era." To allow numerous Japanese immigrants to settle in the United States would be to "cause a race problem and invite and insure a race contest." It was best, he concluded, "to keep them out."[9] To try and make exclusion as palatable as possible to the Japanese, Roosevelt brokered the so-called Gentlemen's Agreement of 1907 in which the United States agreed to refrain from exclusively anti-Japanese legislation in return for a promise from the Japanese government to cease the issuance of passports to allow Japanese workers to immigrate to the United States.

The agreement temporarily removed one source of animosity between the United States and Japan, but it did little or nothing to quiet the growing opinion in America that the nation (and the world) was on the verge of a racial crisis and that the Japanese were becoming the foremost leaders of the frightening "yellow peril." Homer Lea's 1909 book, *The Valor of Ignorance*, suggested that Japan was on the verge of a violent wave of military expansionism and that in just a short time it would challenge the United States for supremacy in the Far East. Many readers in America dismissed the study as nonsense; notions of the Japanese militarily defeating the United States seemed preposterous. But after Japan's victories over China and Russia, not everyone was so certain, and the book sold thousands of copies.

In 1916 the American eugenicist Madison Grant published *The Passing of the Great Race*. The book was little short of a diatribe on race suggesting that the attributes of the various races were constant and unchanged by nature or any force for that matter. American democracy, Grant declared, was endangered not only by the hordes of "undesirable" (i.e., non-Anglo-Saxon) immigrants but also by the lamentable "sentimentality" exhibited by some Americans who tried to protect the "weak, the broken, and the mentally crippled of all races" who managed to "swarm" into the United States. It was left to Lothrop Stoddard, a Harvard-educated racist, to pull all of these threads together. Published in 1922, *The Rising Tide of Color Against White World Supremacy* was nearly hysterical as it described the threat posed to the white world by such a "rising tide." Stoddard began his study with a quote from an article he wrote in 1914, prior to the outbreak of World War I. At that time, he believed that, "The world-wide struggle between the primary races of mankind—the 'conflict of color,' as it has been happily termed—bids fair to be the fundamental problem of the twentieth century, and great communities like the United States of America, the South African Confederation, and Australasia regard the 'color question' as perhaps the gravest problem of the future." The aftermath of the Great War, during which the white races, weakened by the cataclysm of war, faced a growing and increasingly aggressive "tide" of people of color from around the world, only exacerbated his concerns. The world was very much changed. "What a transformation! Instead of a world politically nine-tenths white, we see a world of which only four-tenths at the most can be considered predominantly white in blood, the rest of the world being inhabited mainly by the other primary races of mankind—yellows, browns, blacks, and reds." The most numerous were the "yellows." Of these, the Japanese were of most concern to Stoddard. "Japan was the first yellow people to go methodically to the white man's school," mastering his technology and stratagems in its victories over China and Russia. Stoddard was convinced that these were merely the beginning stages of a Japanese plan for complete control of the Far East. As he explained, "This Japanese programme looks first to the prevention of all further white encroachment in the Far East by the establishment of a Far Eastern Monroe Doctrine based on Japanese predominance and backed if possible by the moral support of the other Far Eastern peoples. The next stage in Japanese foreign policy seems to be the systematic elimination of all existing white holdings in the Far East." Most ominously for Stoddard, Japan's successes were breeding dangerous ideas among the people of color of the world. Its successes against Russia in 1904–1905 were of the utmost importance, he argued.

> The upshot was the Russo-Japanese War of 1904, an event the momentous character of which is even now not fully appreciated. Of course, that war was merely the sign-manual of a whole nexus of forces making for a revivified Asia. But it dramatized and clarified ideas which had been germinating half-unconsciously in millions of colored minds, and both Asia and Africa thrilled with joy and hope. Above all, the legend of white invincibility lay, a fallen idol, in the dust. Nevertheless, though freed from imaginary terrors, the colored world accurately gauged the white man's practical strength and appreciated the magnitude of the task involved in overthrowing white supremacy. That supremacy was no longer acquiesced in as inevitable and hopes of ultimate success were confidently entertained.[10]

Despite the palpable note of panic in Stoddard's book, by the time it appeared it was already clear that white supremacy would not die an easy death. Nor, despite the confidence of the "colored world," was it at all clear that "ultimate success" lay at hand.

During World War I Japan joined the Allies—Great Britain, France, Russia (until 1917), and the United States (which entered the fray in 1917). The foremost goal of the Japanese was to seize control of German holdings in China and the Pacific, but Japan also contributed its large and powerful navy to protecting Allied shipping from German raiders and even sent several ships into the Mediterranean to assist the British navy. The Japanese government's representatives went to the Versailles Peace Conference in 1919 confident that their territorial acquisitions would be recognized and that their nation's status as a great power would be ensured. They also carried with them a resolution demanding that a statement of racial equality be included in the final peace settlement.

The Japanese racial equality resolution is little remembered or discussed in most studies of the peace conference ending World War I. Some scholars attempt to dismiss the episode as a disingenuous scheme by the Japanese to deflect criticism of their territorial demands by putting forward a proposal they knew would be little short of explosive; the theory being that to force acceptance of their demands for German holdings in the Far East, the Japanese would offer to pull the racial equality proposal from the table. Historian Paul Gordon Lauren, who has carried out the most extensive study of the racial equality proposal at Versailles, finds little solid evidence to back up those contentions.[11] In fact, his analysis of the Japanese negotiating position at the conference suggests quite convincingly that the Japanese government and people were strongly committed to the racial equality resolution. Having endured years of anti-Japanese racism, Western suspicion and patronizing attitudes, and "gentlemen's agreements" that effectively barred Japanese immigrants from the United States, Japan had come to believe that its claims to great power status would never be fully recognized until racial equality was accepted at the international level.

At least initially, the Japanese at Versailles entertained the hope that their resolution might be accepted. Much of that faith rested on the shoulders of the man who chaired the conference deliberations—President Woodrow Wilson. Wilson's rhetoric before, during, and after the war suggested that he might be supportive of the notion of racial equality. He spoke often of how the war would make the world "safe for democracy." In a number of speeches and interviews he hammered home the point that a true and lasting peace would only emerge when all nations—large and small, powerful and weak—were considered as equals on the international stage. The Japanese, however, horribly misread Wilson and his policies on race. Born and raised a southerner, Wilson nurtured strong racial prejudices his entire life. Upon becoming the U.S. president in 1913, he almost immediately issued a presidential order directing that all federal offices in Washington, D.C., be racially segregated. When the brutally racist film *Birth of a Nation* was released in 1915, Wilson had it shown in the White House on a number of occasions, declaring that viewing the movie was like watching "history written with lightening." The movie's lurid portrayal of what happened in the South when the former slaves were granted rights and the vote—massive corruption, gross inefficiency, and most troubling, sexual predations against white women—resonated with Wilson and many other Americans who had begun to seriously question whether racial inferiors could ever live alongside whites in peace and harmony. So-called scientific racism (one of the English language's great oxymorons) was at its zenith in the United States, with scholars avidly studying blood, language, facial structure, skin color, intelligence, and—of course—that old mainstay of the racial sciences, human skulls to discern the innate differences between the races of man. Relying on wild bastardizations of Darwin's theories, they created "family trees" for humanity, with visual aids indicating the rise of man from the lowly ape to the civilized Anglo-Saxon. As their theories suggested, some varieties of humankind remained "stuck" on lower-hanging limbs—"missing links" between apes and man. Wilson's cultural background made him particularly receptive to such theories.

Even had Wilson been more personally receptive to the ideal of racial equality, he would have found himself severely constrained by domestic and international forces. At home, violence against African Americans reached near fever pitch in the months after World War I. Episodes of lynching rose dramatically and the Ku Klux Klan, which had been dormant since the 1890s, began to reemerge and recruit more followers. In such a climate, Wilson would have been hard-pressed to argue for racial equality on a global scale. Furthermore, the American president was under pressure from his white colleagues at the conference. Great Britain and Australia were the most vociferous opponents of the Japanese proposal. Australia's prime minister announced that his own position on allowing Japanese into his nation was "Slap the Japs!" Many of the British delegates shared the same rough racist outlook, but their concerns ran deeper. As the foremost colonial power in the world, Great Britain was reluctant to acknowledge that its native "charges" in Africa and Asia were, in fact, racial equals.

Not surprisingly, therefore, the Japanese proposal met stiff resistance when it came up at the negotiations. The British and Wilson attempted to placate Japan by offering up watered-down versions of a racial equality resolution. The Japanese bristled, insisted that the resolution be included in the covenant for the proposed League of Nations, and then pushed their proposal forward to a vote. Despite the protestations of Wilson, Great Britain, and Australia, the resolution passed relatively easily with eleven (including China) in favor and six against. Before the Japanese could celebrate their victory, however, Wilson announced that because the proposal had not received unanimous support and because of the "too serious objections on the part of some of us" (meaning the Anglo-Saxon bloc) the motion failed. Even some of Wilson's supporters were stunned, for this was the first time during the deliberations that unanimity was a requirement for passage of a motion. The president's arguments did not fool the Japanese, who were outraged by Wilson's parliamentary shenanigans. The impact was clear, however: international racial equality was a dead issue at Versailles.

Still stinging from the rebuke in 1919, just two years later the Japanese joined the other great powers in Washington to discuss a variety of issues, including limitations on the construction of warships. The Washington Naval Conference of 1921–22 marked another in the string of what the Japanese perceived as racist slights from the West. The final proceedings resulted in a number of agreements, including the Five-Power Naval Limitation Treaty. Each of the five signatories (the United States, Great Britain, Japan, France, and Italy) agreed to the maintenance of a ratio in terms of each nation's warships. But the Japanese were disgruntled at the proposed ratio: United States—5; Great Britain—5; Japan—3. Soon the story circulated that the Japanese were privately referring to the ratios as "Cadillac: Rolls: Ford." American and British arguments that their nations must maintain navies in both the Atlantic and Pacific while the Japanese were basically a Pacific power did not assuage Japan's suspicions that the Anglo-American bloc was conspiring to limit its power. Japan received another slap in the face when in 1924 the United States drastically revised its immigration laws, tossed out the Gentlemen's Agreement, and virtually excluded the Japanese as "preferred" immigrants to America. (Not surprisingly, Madison Grant eagerly provided his pseudoscientific "evidence" of the inferiority of Asians and other races to the U.S. Congress in support of the legislation.)

The defeat of the racial equality resolution at Versailles, the dismissal of Japanese claims to great power equality at the Washington conference, and the stigma of the 1924 immigration legislation combined to convince the hard-line, militarist, and expansionist elements of the Japanese government that negotiations with the West—and particularly the United States—were useless. By the 1930s Japan adopted a more aggressive posture, attacking China in 1931 and withdrawing from the five-power agreement in 1934. U.S.-Japanese relations rapidly deteriorated, and in December 1941 the Japanese attacked the U.S. naval base at Pearl Harbor in Hawaii. After the attack, faced with a people who were more than a mere curiosity or annoyance, Americans took a keener interest in trying to define the nature of the Japanese. Older "yellow peril" stereotypes were refurbished and reinvigorated, and new "scientific" studies of the Japanese were undertaken.

The war in the Pacific, as John Dower notes in his magisterial study, *War Without Mercy*, was infused with racist perceptions on both sides.[12] In Japanese propaganda, Americans were often depicted as buffoonish, weak, and decadent individuals, and in many Japanese cartoons, Americans were transformed into demons and devils. For the United States, decades of increasing animosity toward Japan, which was often exacerbated by racism, created a situation whereby the conflict with the Japanese acquired overtones absent from the simultaneous battles against Nazi Germany and Fascist Italy. First and foremost, when characterizing the German or Italian enemies, Americans often resorted to personifying them in the form of Adolf Hitler or Benito Mussolini. Aside from occasional references to the emperor or a major military figure such as Hidecki Tojo, the United States generally considered the Japanese en masse—a faceless, nameless horde lacking any sense of individuality. In addition, while some Americans thought that the German and Italian people had simply been misled by charismatic demagogues and that there might indeed be "good" and "bad" Germans and Italians, no such differentiation existed when the United States viewed the Japanese. "A Jap is a Jap," as one U.S. military official put it: all of them savages, all of them warlike, all of them bent on the destruction of the United States. Strong evidence of that viewpoint was the resurgent interest in Homer Lea's nearly forgotten *The Valor of Ignorance*, which was reprinted in 1942 and hammered home the point that all Japanese adhered to a single viewpoint.

Once the United States was at war with Japan, any lingering notions that the Japanese were a "different" kind of Asian or that they represented a more "civilized" Asian vanished. So, too, did any reluctance to express derogatory, racist opinions about the people of Japan for fear of antagonizing a potential enemy. During the war a dizzying variety of racial stereotypes appeared (or simply surfaced). Again and again, the physical size of Japanese people was accentuated. Inevitably, the Japanese were referred to as "little," their very stature denoting their rank in terms of human development. Despite the staggering success of the Japanese attack on Pearl Harbor, myths developed about their inability to see at night and to the difficulty they had flying planes, which was caused by the shape of their skulls and inner ear canals. Editorial cartoons quickly adopted a catchall portrayal of the typical Japanese: wildly exaggerated slanted eyes; thick glasses (the sight problem, again); and huge, protruding buckteeth. Even Theodor Seuss Geisel (more popularly known as Dr. Seuss), who drew numerous editorial cartoons during the war, could not refrain from using these attributes in his drawings of the Japanese. The final physical aspect that came to instantly denote the Japanese was their skin color. Yellow was easily connected with other terms: "yellowbellies," "yellow bastards," "little yellow fellows." For Americans, yellow denoted cowardice, and after the surprise attack on Pearl Harbor, it seemed entirely appropriate that the Japanese were "yellow" people.

Very often, however, the Japanese were simply reduced to subhuman status in American newspapers, magazines, and speeches. They were "savages," "barbarians," or "beasts." The most popular icons to identify the Japanese were vermin and monkeys. The Japanese appeared in thousands of editorial cartoons as fleas, roaches, or—the most popular—rats. The use of vermin to denote the Japanese fit in well with the overall perception of the Japanese as a mindless, vicious, unclean horde. When depicted as monkeys, the Japanese were either hulking, drooling apes or comical chimpanzees swinging through the trees. As famous war correspondent Ernie Pyle noted, the effect of all of these images was to create in the American mind the idea that the "Japanese were looked upon as something subhuman and repulsive; the way some people feel

World War II propaganda poster that manages to use just about every popular stereotype about the Japanese: pidgin English, obsequious politeness, buckteeth (with some viperlike fangs added in), massive eyeglasses (part of the popular American belief that the Japanese as a people had poor eyesight), pointed demonlike ears, general ratlike visage, and the innate bloodthirstiness and untrustworthiness of the Japanese signified by the dagger dripping blood. Source: Poster, NWDNS-179-WP-1186, "Tokio Kid," ca. 1942–1943, War Production Board, 1942–1943, Records of the War Production Board, 1918–1947, Record Group 179, Still Picture Records LICON, Special Media Archives Services Division (NWCS-S), National Archives, College Park, MD.

about cockroaches or mice." His own experience with the Japanese did not shake that feeling. After watching some of the Japanese prisoners of war behaving "just like normal human beings," Pyle admitted, "And yet they gave me the creeps, and I wanted a mental bath after looking at them."[13]

Because of their national heritage Japanese Americans were lumped in with the "enemy." In February 1942 President Franklin Roosevelt issued Executive Order 9066 ordering the evacuation of Japanese and Japanese Americans from the U.S. West Coast. Over 110,000 people were henceforth rounded up by American officials and soldiers and sent to concentration camps where they could be watched and controlled. The public reason for such a drastic action was that these individuals posed a security risk to America. No such risk was ever proved, and in fact security played only a small part in the government's action. The intensity of the anti-Japanese feeling in the wake of Pearl Harbor was terrific. For many, the forced evacuations and incarceration of Japanese Americans simply allowed many Americans to do what they had always wanted to do: remove the offending "yellow" people from American society. Those sent to the camps lost millions of dollars in wages and had their property seized and other assets frozen. Congressman John Rankin from Mississippi, a state that knew a thing or two about dealing with "race problems," applauded the actions. "Once a Jap, always a Jap. You can't more regenerate a Jap than you can reverse the laws of nature." Apparently, the same was not true for Germans and Italians. Their descendants in the United States were not herded behind barbed wire.

World War II, however, made for strange bedfellows. While castigating the Japanese as barbaric animals and playing the "yellow peril" threat to the hilt, the United States faced a bit of a dilemma. Allied with America against the Japanese was China—the home of Fu-Manchu. Attempts were made to differentiate the Chinese and Japanese in the American mind (which was somewhat difficult since Asians had always been Asians as far as most Americans were concerned). A short piece in *Time* just two weeks after the attack on Pearl Harbor took the direct approach. The article, entitled "How to Tell Your Friends From the Japs," provided pictures of typical "Japanese" and "Chinese" people. It then listed the salient differences. The Japanese were "short" and were "seldom fat; they often dry up and grow lean as they age." Though the people of both nations had the typical slanted eyes, the Japanese eyes were "usually set closer together" (and, of course, close-set eyes were always a sign that someone was suspicious or hiding something). Chinese individuals appeared "placid, kindly, and open"; the Japanese, in contrast, were "dogmatic" and "arrogant." In addition, the Japanese were "hesitant, nervous in conversation, [and they] laugh loudly at the wrong time." The two peoples even had different walks: the Japanese "walk stiffly erect, hard heeled"; the Chinese were "more relaxed, have an easy gait, sometimes shuffle."[14]

Somewhat more indirectly, the U.S. government retreated ever so slightly from the Chinese Exclusion Act, which had barred Chinese immigrants to America since the late 1800s. Being the only race on the planet singled out as particularly "undesirable" by the United States had always irritated the Chinese, and officials from China used the opportunity of their wartime alliance with America to push for amelioration of the slight as a recognition of China's role as a great power battling the Japanese. The increased racial animosity spawned by the war, however, was not so easily dissipated. Despite the Department of State's argument that the Exclusion Act was an unnecessary and destructive impediment to better relations with China, many congressmen remained unmoved. Debates raised anew the fear of Chinese "hordes" slipping into America, taking jobs, and generally lowering the quality of life. Only severe pressure from the White House broke the impasse, but it was a meager victory. A new immigration ruling in 1943 allowed a grand total of 105 Chinese to enter the country every year. Apparently the Chinese, even this new "placid, kindly, and open" variety, were still persona non grata.

All warfare is terribly brutal and inhumane; the notion of "good" wars fought between "gentlemen" combatants is a scenario created by the writers of "historical fiction." Yet, as Dower graphically describes in his study of the U.S. war against Japan, a quite different kind of war took place in the Pacific. A combination of factors led U.S. forces to adopt policies and practices toward their Asian enemy that would have at an earlier time and against a different foe been unthinkable. The sneak attack on Pearl Harbor was an important component; the fact that the Japanese had carried out the dastardly assault increased the fury of the American people. In addition, stories of Japanese atrocities against American prisoners of war also fanned the flames of hatred. Little remembered is the fact that Germany soon after Pearl Harbor also declared war on the United States and that German atrocities against American prisoners, notably the Malmedy Massacre of December 1944, also took place. Yet, there was never any serious discussion in the American press about annihilating the German people to the last man and woman. Demands for such actions against the Japanese were commonplace. What else was one to do when confronted with vermin but exterminate the nest? The results of this attitude in the Pacific war were varied: a reluctance to take prisoners, torture of wounded and captive Japanese, and a gruesome (and relatively well-known and publicized) proclivity on the part of U.S. servicemen to collect battlefield "souvenirs" (ears, skulls, bones, gold teeth) from dead and wounded Japanese soldiers. The American people seemed to take such actions in stride. "*Life* published a full-page photograph of an attractive blonde posing with a Japanese skull she had been sent" by her boyfriend in the Pacific. Similar atrocities may have occurred in the war in Europe, but if they did, they were not proudly announced to the American public. In short, the war against the Germans and the Italians never reached the furious intensity of the hatred directed toward the Japanese. In Europe, Americans battled "Nazis" or "Fascists." In the Pacific, the United States fought "Japs." When atomic bombs leveled the cities of Nagasaki and Hiroshima, no tears were shed for the thousands of civilians scorched and vaporized in an instant or for the many more who suffered lingering deaths from radiation poisoning.

In August 1945 the war against Japan came to an end. In somewhat typical fashion, once the Japanese were no longer a threat, the United States came to view them as errant children who now needed remedial education in the areas of democracy, government, and civilization. Americans' anger toward the people of Japan did not disappear overnight, of course, but once the heat of war abated they became more willing to view the actions of the Japanese as what, unfortunately, occurred when an inferior people broke free from the constraints of Western civilization and power. The postwar goal was not annihilation (the Cold War in Asia and the necessity of the recovery of the Japanese economy to help sustain the economic vitality of the region made such thoughts absurd) but "Americanization." The Japanese, after all, had always been good "mimics."

By the time the 1950s rolled around, even that most insidious icon of the "yellow peril," Fu-Manchu, had undergone some transformations. The final entry in the series, *Emperor Fu-Manchu*, appeared in 1959 and lacked the style, breathtaking pace, and focus of the earlier novels. The evil doctor was still up to many of his old tricks—kidnapping helpless westerners, tinkering with poisons, and even raising the dead for an army of zombies. However, his venom (literally and symbolically) was also turned against the communists who now controlled his beloved China. According to Rohmer, Fu-Manchu was "still an enemy to be reckoned with and as menacing as ever, but he has changed with the times. Now he is against the Chinese Communists and, indeed, Communists everywhere, and a friend of the American people."[15] With the defeat of Japan, Stoddard's apocalyptic "rising tide of color" seemed to have crested and ebbed.

CHAPTER 4

BLACK

N **APRIL 18, 1955,** REPRESENTATIVES FROM twenty-nine countries settled in to hear the opening address of the Asian-African
Conference in Bandung, Indonesia. Delegates from India, Thai-
land, Saudi Arabia, North and South Vietnam, Ethiopia, and a score of
other nations, together with reporters, observers from nonparticipant
nations, and curious onlookers listened to the opening address from In-
donesian President Sukarno and heard him declare, "This is the first international conference of colored peoples in the history of mankind."[1]
Sukarno's speech was inspiring and sometimes fiery in its denunciations
of colonialism and racism. Perhaps the most surprising talk delivered
that day, however, came from an unlikely source. As one observer of the
day's proceedings noted, Carlos P. Romulo, chief of the Philippine delegation, had been, "Long heralded as the chief spokesman for the ideas
of the West." This was hardly a surprising assessment. The Philippines
had a long history as a colony first of Spain and then later of the United
States, achieving its independence only in 1946. Even as a sovereign nation, the former U.S. colony was still clearly influenced by the United
States, and some commentators suggested that the country was merely
an American puppet. But instead of the rather equivocating speech most
in the audience were expecting, Romulo cut loose with an impassioned
criticism of white racism. Racial equality, he declared, was the "touch-
stone, I think, for most of us assembled here and the peoples we represent." There had never been a "Western colonial regime" that had not
"imposed, to a greater or lesser degree, on the people it ruled, the doctrine of their own racial inferiority." And then in a particularly powerful
passage, Romulo noted,

73

We have known, and some of us still know, the searing experience of being demeaned in our own lands, of being systematically relegated to subject status not only politically and economically, and militarily—but racially as well. Here was a stigma that could be applied to rich and poor alike, to prince and slave, boss man and workingman, landlord and peasant, scholar and ignoramus. To bolster his rule, to justify his own power to himself, Western white man assumed that his superiority lay in his very genes, in the color of his skin. This made the lowliest drunken sot superior, in colonial society, to the highest product of culture and scholarship and industry among the subject people.

Romulo concluded by observing that "we can only hope that this conference serves as a sober and yet jolting reminder to them that the day of Western racism is passing along with the day of Western power over non-Western peoples. Its survival in any form can only hang like an albatross around the necks of those many people in the West who sincerely seek to build a freer and better world."[2]

Romulo's speech was but one signal of the changing attitudes on race taking hold in the post–World War II period. Even before the war, scientific racism came under assault by much of the scientific community. Led by anthropologists such as Franz Boas, new theories about the influence of culture and society began to displace the older concepts, which concentrated on physical differences to explain the varieties of mankind. The final nail in the coffin for much of the more virulent racism that pseudoscience had supported was provided by the atrocities carried out by the Nazi regime. After 1945 few people wished to be associated with the Aryan supremacist nonsense of Hitler and his followers.

Racism in America, however, did not disappear. Despite the increasing assaults on scientific racism and growing demands for equality from African Americans, the United States remained deeply divided on racial lines. Most African Americans in the South were kept from the ballot box and lived in a Jim Crow society that demeaned them on a daily basis. Lynchings, beatings, and other violence against black Americans were not uncommon occurrences. In short, while racism was no longer a subject for "polite" conversation in the United States, millions of Americans still groaned under its weight.

Nor did the war signal an end to racism's role in America's foreign policy. In the post–World War II period, American racism found itself under assault both at home and abroad. Domestically, the civil rights movement, demanding an end to the second-class citizenship under which African Americans suffered, grew in numbers and in strength. Abroad, America was condemned for its support of the Western imperial powers in their efforts to hold onto or reclaim their colonial empires. It was likewise subjected to scathing criticisms of its racist domestic policies, which suggested to some that U.S. pronouncements about freedom, equality, and justice were mere Cold War rhetoric. As American policymakers discovered to their dismay and confusion, the domestic and international aspects of race and racism were combining in complex and challenging ways. Nowhere was this more apparent than in U.S. dealings with Africa and with African Americans who were demanding a greater voice in America's foreign relations.

I

During most of the nineteenth century, the United States considered Africa a rather uninteresting mystery. In part this was because the United States had few economic interests and even fewer political and strategic interests in the African continent during that period. Race, however, also played a large role in American apathy toward Africa, for Africans were almost unanimously believed to be the lowest, most debased, and most primitive of all non-white peoples.

In some ways, the American disinterest in Africa is surprising. Certainly it can be argued that through the first decades of U.S. existence, Anglo-Saxon Americans had greater contact and interactions with Africans than with Asians or even Latin Americans. The presence of nearly four million black slaves in America by the time of the Civil War in 1861 did not, however, result in an outpouring of curiosity about the lands from which this human property was taken. While American naturalists, artists, and travelers beat a path to Latin America and American traders plied their wares in the Far East, Africa remained almost completely untouched by the United States. Even the establishment of Liberia in 1820 by the American Colonization Society in order to resettle freed slaves did not spark much interest from most white Americans—or many of the freed slaves, for that matter.

In the rankings of race developed in the late 1700s and early 1800s in the United States, blacks were always near or at the very bottom of humanity. Benjamin Franklin, who held a great interest in the varieties of mankind, referred to blacks as having a "plotting Disposition, dark, sullen, malicious, revengeful, and cruel in the highest Degree." As historian Michael Hunt notes, American school textbooks from that period were just as blunt in dealing with the Africans: "They are a brutish people, having little more of humanity but the form."[3] Dr. Samuel George Morton's skull measurements consistently placed Africans at the very bottom of human development. By the time Josiah Nott was spewing his viewpoints about race mixing and arguing that slavery was the natural lot of the inferior Africans, most Americans, from the North and South, agreed that the natives of Africa were examples of the lowest form of the human race. Little wonder, then, that Americans showed little or no interest in investigating the African continent for themselves.

The American experience with Haiti also helped in squelching interest in how Africans might exist apart from their existence as slaves. The United States kept a nervous eye on the French colony of Saint Domingue and watched in horror as a government composed of former black African slaves proclaimed the independence of the new nation they now christened Haiti in January 1804. Among white Americans, particularly southern slaveholders, the Haitian revolution was viewed with concern and disgust. It was not until 1862, during America's Civil War, that the United States extended diplomatic recognition to the "black republic." Nevertheless, the nation attracted little attention from the American government aside from observations on the backwardness and brutishness of Haitian society. In 1915, however, when another revolution shook Haiti, the United States decided that the unruly Haitians needed a lesson in how to govern themselves. President Woodrow Wilson and Secretary of State William Jennings Bryan, claiming that anarchy in the island nation threatened hemispheric stability and U.S. investments, ordered the Marines to occupy Haiti. Bryan had little knowledge of the nation and requested a briefing from an American businessman familiar with Haiti. Bryan's first response to a presentation on the nation's history, society, and politics was, "Dear me, imagine that! Niggers speaking French." During the first years of the American occupation, thousands of Haitians were killed in battles with U.S. forces. Not until 1934 did the Marines depart, and once again Haiti faded from American interest.

In the latter part of the nineteenth century and the early years of the twentieth, however, Americans suddenly discovered Africa. More correctly, they invented an Africa—the "dark continent" full of savages, lust, and adventure. The man most responsible for "opening" Africa to the American public was journalist Henry Morton Stanley, who traveled there in 1871 under the auspices of the *New York Herald* on an expedition to look for the "lost" missionary, David Livingstone. With the famous phrase "Dr. Livingstone, I presume?" Stanley secured his place in history by locating the old and ailing doctor. Stanley quickly capitalized on his fame by writing a number of books, all of which became bestsellers, detailing his travels in Africa. In general, Stanley's description of the Africans was less virulently racist than might have been expected from a late-nineteenth-century American. However, he left no doubt about the absolutely primitive state of the natives he encountered. They were "a people just emerged into the Iron Epoch, and now thrust forcibly under the notice of nations who have left them behind by the improvements of over 4000 years." The Africans were "still fixed deeply in barbarism."[4]

Former President Theodore Roosevelt also did his part to bring Africa to the American people. He wrote about his 1909 expedition to Africa, which he used as an excuse to open fire on nearly anything that walked, crawled, or flew for "scientific" study. As had Stanley, Roosevelt placed the Africans themselves far back on the historical continuum. The "wildlife" in Africa—both animal and human—"does not differ materially from what it was in Europe in the late Pleistocene." This comparison was anything but "fanciful," according to the former Rough Rider, for what one saw in Africa "substantially reproduces the conditions of life in Europe as it was . . . ages before the dawn of anything that could be called civilization."[5]

As popular as the writings of Stanley and Roosevelt became, they paled in comparison to the much wider readership achieved by Edgar Rice Burroughs with his Tarzan novels. The first in the Tarzan series appeared in 1912 and set the stage for those that followed. The "ape man" Tarzan was actually an Englishman of noble heritage who had been orphaned in the jungles of Africa. Raised by the apes, and taking on the name Tarzan, he nevertheless rejected much of the savagery and barbarism of the black Africans with whom he came in contact. Instead, what Burroughs referred to as his "hereditary instinct" led Tarzan to teach himself to read and write, to abstain from cannibalism, and to protect white women from the predations of primitive Africans. As pulp fiction, the Tarzan stories naturally exaggerated to absurd levels the negative perceptions most Americans already had of Africa and the people that inhabited the continent. Africa got even darker, more dangerous, and violent in Burroughs's novels, and the sexual overtones therein sometimes reached near hysterical levels. The basic premise of the series was always clear: even when subjected to an environment of barbaric primitivism, a white man would rise above his surroundings and bring the light of civilization to the darkest jungles. Once the Tarzan movies began to flood theaters, stereotypical Africa was soundly imprinted on the minds of many

Americans as a land of dense and forbidding jungles, ferocious (and always man-eating) animals, natives who swung between comical superstition and horrifying savagery, and above all, a sense that Africa was a place (and the Africans a people) left frozen in time many thousands of years before.

Yet, despite the entertainment value of Africa for American readers and moviegoers, the continent remained of little official concern to U.S. policymakers. Total U.S. trade with Africa in the year before the outbreak of World War I was a mere fifty million dollars, with Egypt and South Africa accounting for nearly half of that amount. American trade with Oceania, in comparison, was nearly twice as high. A major reason for the lack of economic (and political) contact was the fact that Africa, in truth, barely existed. Instead, there were British Africa, French Africa, Portuguese Africa, Belgian Africa, and German Africa. In the late 1800s the continent had been sliced, divided, and apportioned among the European powers. America was left out of these negotiations but was relatively untroubled by the Europeans' action. By that time, the United States was concentrating on the "great China market." By 1939 total trade with the continent increased to nearly one hundred million dollars—which was still less than total U.S. trade with the Netherlands.[6] Africa barely registered on America's diplomatic radar.

World War II temporarily awakened America to the existence of Africa. U.S. soldiers fought and died in North Africa. African natural resources, such as rubber from Liberia, were essential to the war effort. And in a global struggle, African ports and airbases took on new significance. As the war drew to a close, however, Africa returned to its usual position on the back burner of U.S. foreign policy interests. With war-ravaged Europe and Asia as areas of first priority, the "dark continent" once again slipped into diplomatic obscurity. The English, the French, the Portuguese, and the other European colonialists could handle African affairs.

The Cold War, which erupted shortly after the end of World War II, first served as a further impetus toward the diplomatic irrelevance of Africa for American officials. In the post–World War II world, the biggest problem areas were in Europe and the Far East, with China teetering on the brink of falling into the communist camp. Since the Soviets seemed to initially have as little interest in Africa as the United States, it was readily put at the bottom of the diplomatic pecking order. It did not take long, however, for the Cold War to have the exact opposite effect, and in just a few years, Africa took on new and concrete importance for the United States. As always, race hovered in the background of this new American interest.

When the Soviet Union began to take a more active interest in Africa—and the rest of the third world—in the mid-1950s, American interest also increased. Part of the reason for a more focused U.S. take on the underdeveloped nations of Africa, Asia, and elsewhere was the obvious weakening of the European colonial regimes. World War II was a serious blow to the European imperialists' power and prestige. In addition, the wartime rhetoric of freedom and self-government, such as was found in the famous Atlantic Charter put together by President Franklin Roosevelt and British Prime Minister Winston Churchill, helped to encourage anticolonial rebellions in Africa and Asia. Coinciding with this lessening of the European hold on Africa was a growing realization among U.S. officials that the continent was home to some very valuable and necessary resources. The literal jewel in the crown was South Africa, with its supplies of diamonds, gold, and—of particular importance in the atomic age—uranium. Add in fears of Soviet efforts to gain a toehold in Africa, and the stage was set for a dramatic increase in U.S. interest. In a remarkably short period of time, Africa suddenly acquired new importance as a battleground in the Cold War.

Dealing with the African independence movements of the 1950s posed a distinct problem for American officials. Unable or unwilling to shake off their old perceptions of Africa as a primitive backwater, these officials proved extremely reluctant to embrace the anticolonial spirit sweeping through the "dark continent." The African, according to a National Security Council report in 1957, was "still immature and unsophisticated." In response to pleas for assistance from African nationalists, the United States adopted a standard line, as best expressed by Assistant Secretary of State for Near Eastern, South Asian, and African Affairs Henry Byroade in 1953:

> The policies of the United States Government towards colonial questions have not always been clearly understood. Our basic policy, however, is relatively simple. We believe in eventual self-determination for all peoples, and we believe that evolutionary development to this end should move forward with minimum delay. Our Government must approach colonial questions in terms of the enlightened self-interest of the United States. There are regions where human beings are unable to cope with disease, famine, and other forces of nature. Premature independence for these peoples would not serve

the interests of the United States nor the interests of the free
world as a whole.[7]

"Eventual self-determination" and "evolutionary development" were the
keynotes of American policy toward Africa. "Premature independence"
for such an "immature and unsophisticated" people would only lead to
chaos and anarchy, which the wily communists would certainly turn to
their advantage. Such language smacked of the earlier evaluations of the
African continent as a land and peoples thousands of years behind the
rest of humanity and of a general acceptance of the value of white rule
over such a prehistoric region.

Despite brief blips of a more sympathetic U.S. policy toward
Africa during the Kennedy and Johnson years (a sympathy that was more
rhetorical than actual), things did not change much by the 1970s. Anti-
African statements were commonplace during the Nixon presidency, as
has been documented most carefully by Seymour Hersh. Nixon's deputy
assistant for national security affairs Alexander Haig would pretend to
play tom-tom drums when African matters were discussed and would ask
individuals making reports on Africa, "Where's your pet ape?" President
Nixon himself could be the most brutal in his statements. He suggested
to National Security Advisor Henry Kissinger that in a forthcoming speech
he "make sure there's something in it for the jigs." Later, when Kissinger
and Nixon were discussing African affairs, Nixon simply dismissed the
entire continent, saying, "Henry, let's leave the niggers to Bill [Secretary
of State William Rogers] and we'll take care of the rest of the world."[8]

South Africa, however, was where the issues of politics, Cold
War, and race came to a head more concretely and distinctly in America's
foreign relations. The American relationship with the apartheid regime in
South Africa, implemented after the National Party gained power in 1948,
proved troublesome and contradictory, to say the least. The Cold War
implications of the controversial relationship were rather easy to understand. U.S. officials considered South Africa to be the most important
and valuable nation in Africa. Its extraordinary amount of rich natural
resources, coupled with its strategic location, certainly explained why the
United States would want to keep it out of the communist camp. Yet,
these political factors only partially explained the often-tortured stance
American policymakers adopted toward the odious racism of the apartheid system. It was clear that many U.S. officials linked political instability
in Africa with the racial makeup of the native population. When African
Americans and others raised criticisms against the government's apparent support of European colonialism and South Africa's apartheid re-

gime, a familiar response was given. As one key State Department official put it, Africa would be a "fertile field for communism" should there be "premature independence for primitive, underdeveloped peoples."[9]

Throughout the post–World War II period, the American government expressed "concern" about the situation in South Africa. With the Cold War heating up, American trade and investment in South Africa increasing by leaps and bounds, and deep-seated fears about the capability of black South Africans to rule themselves, concern was about as far as Washington was willing to go. There was, however, another factor at work in the American reluctance to criticize the regime in Pretoria. When in 1960 a United Nations resolution condemning apartheid in South Africa was being considered, President Dwight Eisenhower reflected on America's position in the ongoing debate. He felt that "while we, the United States, were trying to better condition [*sic*], he could not escape the feeling that we [were] not entirely in a different position ourselves." If the United States were to "vote for a tough resolution, we may find ourselves red-faced—in other words concerning our own Negro problem."[10] As the old saying goes, people in glass houses should not throw stones. A nation in which millions of its black citizens were denied even the most basic civil rights could hardly be expected to sling mud at South Africa's apartheid.

As world disgust with the racist regime in South Africa grew concurrent with the development of a more active and vocal U.S. civil rights movement, the American government occasionally voiced its "concern" or "regret" over apartheid. Neither the Kennedy nor the Johnson administration, however, took any concrete or effective actions to promote change in South Africa beyond occasional (and often partial) arms embargoes. In the United Nations, the American representatives combined rhetoric that stressed equality and freedom with opposition to sanctions and direct condemnations of the South African government. When Richard Nixon came into office in 1969, his administration simply dispensed with the rhetoric and began what came to be known as a policy "tilt" toward not only South Africa's white government but also the colonial Portuguese regimes still clinging to power in Africa. National Security Advisor Henry Kissinger helped to oversee this process and the preparation of National Security Study Memorandum 39 in 1969. One of the policy options proposed for dealing with white regimes in Africa (derisively referred to as the "tar baby" option by critics in the Department of State) was to establish closer relations with white governments. As the report noted, "the whites are here to stay and the only way that constructive change can come about is through them." It therefore suggested a "selective relaxation of our stance against the white regimes" and a more cooperative attitude toward working with South Africa. As historian Thomas Noer finds, the Nixon administration wasted no time in implementing this "tilt," appointing a new ambassador to South Africa who "ingratiated himself to the South Africans by being the only foreign representative at the opening of a segregated theater and by joining a hunting trip on Robben Island with black prisoners serving as beaters."[11]

In many ways, the Nixon-Kissinger "tilt" was hardly surprising. American policy had never really tilted *against* the white regimes in Africa because U.S. officials were not convinced that the black Africans were capable of self-government. The blatantly racist comments of Nixon administration officials were hardly the norm, but they did reflect a deeply held lack of respect for and interest in the African continent that had been the basis for U.S. policy for decades. In the more "politically correct" post–World War II period, of course, American policymakers denied that race played a role in the rather tepid response to white rule in Africa. The American policy, they explained, was simply based on pragmatism—the white regimes were stable, friendly, and anticommunist. Yet, against the broader background of historic U.S. attitudes toward Africa and its inhabitants, one could easily read that another way: American policy was based on the common assumption that black regimes were unstable, unfriendly, and easy prey for the crafty communists.

II

The United States was not invited to the Bandung Conference, but a number of Americans attended, including the famous African-American author Richard Wright. Upon hearing of the gathering, Wright felt an overwhelming necessity to go to Indonesia and witness what would take place. He felt he, better than most Americans, could understand. "I'm an American Negro; as such, I've had a burden of race consciousness." As he watched the proceedings, the racial meaning of Bandung became apparent to Wright. The attendees, he believed, "began to sense their combined strength; they began to taste blood. . . . They could now feel that their white enemy was far, far away." Their colors mingled together. "Day after day dun-colored Trotskyites consorted with dark Moslems, yellow Indo-Chinese hobnobbed with brown Indonesians, black Africans mingled with swarthy Arabs, tan Burmese associated with dark brown Hindus, dusty nationalists palled around with yellow Communists, and Socialists talked to Buddhists. But they all had the same background of colonial experience, of subjection, of color consciousness." While most American newspapers and magazines accentuated the fact that the communist Chinese were at Bandung, Wright came to another conclusion.

> Bandung was no simple exercise in Left and Right politics; it was no mere minor episode in the Cold War; it was no Communist Front meeting. . . . Bandung was a decisive moment in the consciousness of 65 per cent of the human race, and that moment meant: HOW SHALL THE HUMAN RACE BE ORGANIZED?[12]

For many years, the organization of the human race posed no difficulties for the United States. Racial differences did not mingle together for white America; rather these differences stood humans in stark contrast to each other and established their rank in the hierarchy of race. All of that was coming to an end.

For American policymakers, the postwar years marked a complete unsettling of the old racial notions upon which much of the American empire had been built. The very bases of racism were under attack, and people—the brown, the yellow, and the black—were rising up to successfully challenge white rule around the globe. Suddenly, racial precepts such as Anglo-Saxon superiority and the innate inferiority of other races were no longer advantages in the American push for power and success. To the amazement of U.S. officials, their nation's own racism now became a diplomatic albatross tied securely around the American neck. A world that had been—quite literally—black and white for so many years was turning upside down. American racism was on the defensive around the world.

A 1953 report by an attendee of the Psychological Warfare School at Fort Bragg in North Carolina summarized the situation in no uncertain terms. The Soviets, it declared, were busily at work among the restless people of color around the world. "Soviet propagandists have capitalized on this unrest, stirring up hatreds and creating new ones." America's domestic racism made it the "principal victim" of communist propaganda. As the report concluded, "America's treatment of its Negro minority has been an Achilles heel, and needlessly so."[13] While this report was certainly dramatic, it in fact merely highlighted a situation U.S. policymakers had faced since the end of World War II. The rise of nationalism and demands for independence among the colonized peoples of Asia, Africa, and elsewhere, combined with the apparent eagerness of the Soviets to take advantage of this situation, meant that the rules of the international game had changed. No longer could the United States simply rely on the European powers to "handle" their colonies. As the spirit of independence rose among the colonized peoples and European power waned, it became obvious that America would now have to readjust its attitudes toward the concept of race. It would be necessary to deal with the black, brown, and yellow peoples of the world on a more or less equal basis if the United States wished to count on their assistance in the Cold War.

As poll after poll suggested, however, the biggest impediment the United States faced in gaining the allegiance of the colored masses of the world was its own very ugly and very public race problem. Among the peoples of Africa, Asia, and Latin America, one fact was apparent. While the United States was admired for its accomplishments in the fields of economic growth and prosperity, military might, and political strength, the race issue consistently stuck out like a sore thumb. Almost as disturbing was the fact that even among America's stalwart European allies, the race problem in the United States was beginning to raise serious questions about America's self-proclaimed status as "leader of the free world." How could a nation that watched as millions of its citizens were systematically deprived of their most basic civil rights really be taken seriously when it slammed the Soviet Union for its lack of democracy and freedom?

And as U.S. officials were well aware, the Soviets were certainly making hay with the race issue. America's domestic racism problem was a consistent element in Soviet propaganda, particularly in Asia and Africa. The United States was portrayed as a viciously racist nation, infested with members of the Ku Klux Klan and deserving of grave suspicions from any person of color. When U.S. representatives at the United Nations decried the lack of freedom in elections in communist-controlled Poland or Hungary, the standard response from the Soviets was devastatingly effective: How many black Americans were allowed to vote in South Carolina or Mississippi?

The initial U.S. response was simply to downplay the Soviet propaganda, arguing that the race problem in America was nowhere near as bad as the Soviets portrayed. This approach assumed, of course, that the communists were spreading wild tales and gross lies. No doubt the Soviets engaged in exaggeration when commenting on America's race problem, but it soon became clear that merely denying that a problem existed was a less than effective answer. For one thing, this approach denied what anyone with eyes could see. All one had to do to find news of the latest racist outrage—a lynching, a beating, a bombing—was pick up an American newspaper. When several black children attempted to attend an all-white high school in Little Rock, Arkansas, in 1957, for example, the violent reaction of local whites was so vehement that it was soon featured on front pages around the globe. For another, as more and more African and Asian nations gained their independence, they naturally sent their diplomatic representatives to live and work in Washington, D.C. What these representatives discovered was a segregated city, surrounded by states in which Jim Crow laws were a fact of life. Ugly incidents in which African diplomats were denied housing, had their children denied access to schools, or found themselves unable to use a bathroom or eat at a restaurant along highways in Virginia and Maryland became commonplace.

Exacerbating the situation was the fact that African-American civil rights organizations and leading spokespeople were picking up on the foreign criticisms and using them to their advantage. Linking the battle for civil rights in America with the battles for independence in Africa and Asia, groups such as the National Association for the Advancement of Colored People (NAACP) were quick to suggest that the most effective answer to the charges being raised against the United States would be strong and meaningful civil rights legislation. Walter White, Roy Wilkins, W. E. B. Du Bois, and Paul Robeson lacerated American hypocrisy, which praised freedom with one hand and deprived millions of black Americans of it with the other. African-American newspapers kept up a steady stream of fire, cleverly blunting the charge raised by many segregationists that civil rights groups were riddled with communists by suggesting that in fact those organizations were the best line of defense against Soviet propaganda.[14]

Since denial had proven to be an ineffective defense against charges of racial prejudice against its African-American citizens, the U.S. government embarked on a three-pronged approach to blunting these international (and domestic) criticisms. The first prong was a program to make use of African Americans as official ambassadors for the American way of life. African-American diplomats were a rare commodity in the U.S. foreign policymaking bureaucracy before World War II. Blatant racial bias kept most black Americans from even entering the diplomatic service. Those who persevered found themselves limited to a small number of foreign postings—Liberia, Madagasgar, the Azores—which quickly came to be known as the "Negro circuit." The first African American to serve as a U.S. ambassador was not appointed until 1949, only three others served in that capacity prior to the 1960s, and all served in African nations. For all intents and purposes, the Department of State remained what black newspapers derisively referred to as the "lily-white club" throughout the Cold War. As the official record makes clear, most of the African-American appointments to high-profile positions were merely token gestures, window dressing to counter communist propaganda that suggested that black Americans did not have equal opportunities. Given the pool of African Americans willing and able to provide their talents and expertise in the service of their government, the period represents a shameful and costly misuse of human resources.

Much easier to accomplish was the second prong of the new approach: a rather large-scale and sophisticated counterpropaganda program in which African Americans were utilized as living symbols of America's commitment to equality and civil rights. Pamphlets, brochures, magazines, and even movies were distributed by the Department of State (and, later, the U.S. Information Agency) celebrating the lives of great African Americans such as Ralph Bunche, Booker T. Washington, and (at least until his politics became too radical for official tastes) Du Bois. In addition, the U.S. government sponsored hundreds of speaking trips and visits to foreign lands by black entertainers, authors, and sports figures. Operatic and concert singer Marian Anderson was a popular figure in the world of entertainment, but U.S. officials quickly discovered that foreign nations seemed to have an insatiable taste for jazz. Therefore, Dizzy Gillespie and Louis Armstrong made several trips abroad to entertain foreign audiences. The play *Porgy and Bess* became a staple in the American government-sponsored program of cultural diplomacy. Sport was also an international language, and the U.S. government sent African-American boxers, track and field stars, and other athletes on tour. The most popular of all was the Harlem Globetrotters basketball team, which combined skill and comedy to thrill overseas spectators.

Last, to supplement the efforts of these official and unofficial ambassadors, the U.S. government resorted to applying pressure to silence the most outspoken African-American critics of U.S. foreign policy. Du Bois found himself under assault by federal officials, who ordered investigations by the Federal Bureau of Investigation. When the great black intellectual attempted to go overseas in 1952, he found his passport revoked. Disappointed and disgusted, Du Bois relocated to Ghana in 1961. Paul Robeson, an entertainer turned activist, was investigated by the House Un-American Activities Committee and actually appeared before the committee in 1955. The hearings and accusations of membership in the Communist Party eventually destroyed Robeson's career. Like Du Bois, Robeson had his passport revoked, though it was eventually returned. Even African Americans who were not living in the United States could find themselves hounded by the American government. Josephine Baker, world-renowned singer, dancer, actress, and activist, moved to France in the 1920s. Yet, when Baker toured Latin America in the early 1950s, Department of State officials went on alert and actually attempted to convince governments in the region to deny her entrance to their nations.

Token appointments of African-American diplomats, tours and publicity spotlighting black celebrities, and attempts at muzzling the harshest African-American critics were only marginally successful in creating a new and positive international opinion concerning America's race problem. As the world's reaction to the Little Rock crisis of 1957 suggested, efforts designed to minimize or gloss over the civil rights situation in the United States were tenuous at best and could be completely nullified by any new outbreaks of racial bigotry. Pictures of the terrified African-American students in Little Rock, cowering under verbal abuse, spit, and objects thrown by angry whites instantly destroyed any credibility that might have been built up by a Globetrotters' game or a Dizzy Gillespie concert. President Eisenhower belatedly and reluctantly called in the National Guard to protect the black students, but the sight of the students flanked by bayonet-baring troops—just so they could attend school—was not a comforting vision.

The international fallout from Little Rock convinced some in the Eisenhower administration that a different approach was needed. And so at the 1958 World's Fair, held in Brussels, the U.S. government unveiled the "Unfinished Business" exhibit. This certainly represented a novel departure from America's usual propaganda war with the communist bloc. The basic premise of the exhibit was to show first that the United States was strong enough to admit its problems and second that it was trying to solve them. The range of problems presented in the exhibit was narrowed to three: soil erosion, urban crowding, and the big-ticket item, segregation. The setup for "Unfinished Business" was relatively simple. In the first room, visitors were treated to newspaper clippings and photos that in no uncertain terms illustrated the three problem areas. In the second room, a variety of displays informed guests as to the amount of progress being made toward solutions. Finally, the last room allowed visitors to see the ultimate goals. The exhibitors had little trouble finding disturbing print and visual sources to graphically portray America's race problem in the first room of the exhibit. In the second room facts and figures about African-American achievements in the economic, political, social, and educational fields were displayed. And in the final room, a large picture of black and white children playing ring-around-the-rosy served as a touching and human illustration of the goal of a desegregated American society.

As a piece of Cold War propaganda, "Unfinished Business" was an admirable exhibit. Initial reactions from the Europeans who visited were positive; they were struck by America's forthright admission of its problem and its apparent willingness to move toward desegregation. In terms of short-circuiting criticisms from both friend and foe about the nation's race problem—criticisms that were thought to be costly to U.S. dealings and influence with the rest of the world—it was effective. As a truly representative picture of American attitudes about race, however, it failed miserably. Even before the exhibit officially opened, southern congressmen lashed out with particular venom at what they saw as thinly veiled criticisms of the South's Jim Crow society. They were infuriated by a picture that showed a young African-American man dancing with a white woman, and they were positively livid by the time they came to the huge photograph of the multiracial ring-around-the-rosy. Eisenhower, never a champion of civil rights and often an apologist for southern segregation, immediately ordered the exhibit closed for "renovations." When it reopened, the scene of the couple dancing was gone, the newspaper headlines and pictures were crumpled and overlapped so as not to be *too* obvious, and the large picture of the children was shrunk down considerably. This did nothing to mollify the southern representatives who kept up a steady stream of vitriol until Eisenhower, with no small degree of relief, finally closed the exhibit for good. It was a telling moment in the history of racism and U.S. foreign policy. An initiative, which gave every indication of being an effective Cold War tool in the struggle with the Soviet Union, was trumped by the power of American racism.

By the mid-1960s the U.S. government finally responded to the increasing pressures exerted by the civil rights movement at home and the chorus of international criticisms of its race problem abroad and enacted two landmark pieces of legislation: the 1964 Civil Rights Act and the 1965 Voting Rights Act. American Cold War propaganda prominently featured these strides in granting African Americans equal rights. Yet, U.S. officials also came to the conclusion that passing these important acts meant it was no longer necessary to deal with civil rights and race on the international level. As far as they were concerned, America's "race problem" was over. The discovery that they were terribly wrong came not just on the streets of America's inner cities, which exploded in racial violence during the late 1960s, but also in the jungles of Vietnam, where race and U.S. foreign policy again found themselves face to face.

III

The Vietnam War (1965–73) was America's last great war in Asia in the twentieth century. It was a different time against a different enemy, but echoes of the earlier conflicts in the Philippines in the early 1900s and the battle against Japan in the 1940s could certainly be heard. The war in Vietnam was in many ways symbolic of the post–World War II relationship between race and U.S. foreign policy, a conflict in which old racial stereotypes competed with new postwar realities and were complicated by an increasingly assertive African-American voice in American diplomacy.

The intense and palpable racial animosity that existed in the struggle against Japan in World War II was not as apparent in the American war in Vietnam. North Vietnam, after all, had not attacked America, nor did America have a long history of interaction with Vietnam during which racial conflicts might have arisen. In addition, because the United States involved itself in what was essentially a civil war in Vietnam, the *South* Vietnamese became our allies. Race could not really serve as a tool to dehumanize and degrade the "bad" Vietnamese without tainting the "good" Vietnamese, whom we were defending. Public and private attacks on the Vietnamese as an inferior people, therefore, were rare in the United States; there was certainly nothing like the internment of Japanese Americans during World War II.

Nevertheless, traces of the racial stereotypes and hatreds that had shaped American attitudes toward Asia for well over one hundred years were still visible. The Vietnamese—both friends and enemies—were commonly referred to as gooks, dinks, slant-eyes, and slopes by U.S. military and civilian personnel in Vietnam. The very nature of the warfare conducted by the United States—"search-and-destroy" tactics aiming for attrition (killing so many of the enemy that they could not continue the fight)—was tailor-made for brutality and atrocities. A perfect example of this came in March 1968 when American soldiers engaged in an orgy of violence in the South Vietnamese village of My Lai. When the burning, raping, and shooting ended, hundreds of unarmed peasants—mostly women and children—had been slaughtered. Little wonder that the rule of thumb among many American fighting men in Vietnam was the "mere gook rule"—if it's dead, and it's Vietnamese, it's the enemy.

Despite these occasional relapses into the older forms of racism, by the time American soldiers poured into Vietnam the world had

Photo from the My Lai Massacre, March 1968. This poignant picture shows a young Vietnamese boy trying to protect his much younger brother from the marauding American troops who slaughtered nearly four hundred villagers in My Lai. Almost immediately after the photo was taken the two boys were shot and killed. Photo by Ron Haeberle, March 16, 1968, My Lai Collection, The Vietnam Archive, Texas Tech University, Lubbock, TX.

changed dramatically. The attacks on scientific racism launched by Boas and others earlier in the century seemed to have carried the day, and the idea that culture, not biology, was responsible for the differences one saw between various races was generally accepted in most academic circles. With the post–World War II period, after the world had seen the Aryan insanity of the Third Reich and the horrors of the concentration camps were revealed, came the end of the days of comparing skull sizes and compiling charts that showed how close or far away each race was from its ape origins.

Racism, however, is nothing if not remarkably resilient. It had already weathered the obstacles posed by religion and the idea of mono-genesis. And so, now under assault by science, racism discovered a new home in the post–World War II world in the form of "modernization theory." If racism was no longer an acceptable ideology, how was one to explain the "underdevelopment" of nations in Africa, Asia, and Latin America? The answer that came to dominate U.S. officials' discussions centered on the term "modernization." In general, this new theory posited that societies go through stages of economic (and political) development, from "traditional" to more "advanced" societies. There was no denying, however, that some societies seemed stuck on this path toward progress and modernization. The most accepted explanation for this lack of movement toward a higher plane of civilization was that these societies could not break free from their *cultural* backwardness. The inability of these nations and peoples to achieve the high levels of production, consumption, and stability of a modern nation such as the United States was ascribed to several factors, including (1) a colonial legacy of abuse, misuse, and exploitation; (2) backward ideas concerning education, health, and technology; and (3) lack of experience in democratic forms of government. It was not, therefore, the *people* themselves who were to blame; in fact, the theory seemed at face value to challenge a racial interpretation by suggesting that evolution toward "modernization" was a natural process. It was instead the *culture* of these societies that was clogging the highway to progress.

Yet, as one scholar explains, the change in terminology did little to alter the basic perceptions that had always been behind theories of biological inferiority. Geographer James Blaut argues that the theory of "modernization" in effect stated that

> non-Europeans are not racially, but rather culturally backward in comparison to Europeans because of their history; their lesser cultural evolution. And it is for this reason that they are poor. So they must follow, under European guidance and 'tutelage,' the path already trodden by the Europeans as the only means of overcoming backwardness. Non-Europeans were thereby defined as inferior in attained level of achievement, not potential for achievement. This was the real essence of cultural racism.

As Blaut and others have been quick to point out, the distinctions between biological and cultural racism were blurred from the beginning. What explained, for example, the "better" culture of the Europeans? What satisfactorily explained the continuing poverty of third world cultures? If European (or American) "guidance" was the key to modernization, then why had hundreds of years of European (and American) imperialism failed to break the "cultural" logjams and lead these benighted nations to progress? We turn again to Blaut for an explanation of the intrinsic logic of this new cultural racism:

> the superiority of Europeans as individuals of European culture has very, very old roots and, by inference, is natural and fundamental. This proposition accomplished everything that biological racism accomplished and more. . . . It argues, in

essence, that a cultural, not genetic, superiority appeared in the European cultural pool very long ago and, just like genetic superiority, it has led ever since to a great rate of development for Europe and to a level of development which, at each moment in history, is higher than that of non-European cultures.[15]

In short, at the core of modernization lay old ideas about superiority and inferiority. Whether genetic or cultural, racism survived.

And so it was with Vietnam. The Southeast Asian nation seemed to fit the modernization "profile" perfectly. It had a long and bitter colonial heritage. Even President Franklin D. Roosevelt commented that French rule of Vietnam left it in worse shape than the French had found it in. Vietnam was very much a "traditional" society of peasants and villages, beset by poor education and poor health care, with no middle class to speak of and an elite that seemed stuck in the distant past. For Kennedy and Johnson advisor Walt Whitman Rostow, Vietnam was tailor-made for the magic of modernization theory. Rostow was one of the apostles of the theory, having published in 1960 his popular and influential book, *The Stages of Economic Growth: A Non-Communist Manifesto*, in which he postulated that societies go through "stages" of economic development, from "traditional" societies to the mass-consumer societies that characterized the United States and western European nations. It was all simply a matter of pushing the traditional nations along the path of development, to get them to what he called the "takeoff" point to modernization. Even colonialism in a place like Vietnam played a role, as Rostow explained:

> Although imperial powers pursued policies which did not always optimize the development of the preconditions for takeoff, they could not avoid bringing about the transformation in thought, knowledge, institutions and the supply of social overhead capital which moved the colonial society along the transitional path. . . . In any case, the reality of the effective power that went with an ability to wield modern technology was demonstrated and the more thoughtful local people drew appropriate conclusions.[16]

In Vietnam, U.S. officials often talked about "nation building," as though nothing that even vaguely resembled a nation could exist without the infusion of American know-how, technology, resources, and guidance. As the U.S. ambassador to South Vietnam complained, America was attempting "to bring this medieval country into the 20th Century."

Soon, U.S. advisors were undertaking a program to modernize South Vietnam and were "deciding what colors the lights in the fountains should be in downtown Saigon; whether the library and national museum in Saigon should adopt a decimal system; whether the trees in Saigon should be cut down to make way for parking meters." An American congressman compared the U.S.-directed and funded program of resettling South Vietnamese peasants in what were known as "strategic hamlets" to the settlement of America's West: "It ought also to give us some measure of pride that our example has provided the inspiration for this experiment in Vietnam."[17] Apparently, prior to the arrival of the Americans, the Vietnamese peasants had no idea about settling lands and farming them.

Thus, the "modernization" of South Vietnam proceeded with the same time-honored assumptions about the superiority of the Anglo-Saxon race. Instead of putting the argument in biological terms, however, the discussion now revolved around words such as "civilization," "progress," and "culture." As historian Michael Latham puts it, U.S. officials believed that the people of South Vietnam were not drawn to participate in the revolution "out of an allegiance to the larger historical and cultural concept of a united, independent Vietnam or even because of the appeal presented by a promised redistribution of power and wealth in the agrarian social structure. Peasants joined the NLF [the National Liberation Front, usually referred to as the "Viet Cong" by the Americans] simply because they wanted to be like Westerners." In short, the rebels in South Vietnam were not communists, or even nationalists. They simply reflected the rising tide of expectation from a backward and downtrodden people who wanted what Americans had: wealth, abundant consumer goods, and freedom. Unfortunately, they just did not know how to get there. U.S. officials, therefore, facing what they considered the absurd prospect of the Vietnamese ignoring the "stages of economic growth" and attempting to define their own future, "understood their duty as one of helping South Vietnam advance through the volatile period in which social revolution might prevent destined progress." As U.S. officials stressed, however, it was not a matter of race. "Turning toward culture and stressing the essential malleability of the 'traditionals,' American modernizers, like the more optimistic advocates of Indian assimilation and overseas imperialism, carved out another kind of redemptive mission for themselves. The foreign would not fade away, but, under American influence, their deficient cultures would."[18]

For African Americans, this must have all had a rather familiar sound to it. The old American racism seemed to be on the defensive. The combined forces of the attacks on scientific racism and the rise of the civil rights movement were slowly, almost glacially, prompting change. First with John F. Kennedy and then more prominently with Lyndon Baines Johnson, the domestic fight over racism took on the same tones being used in the modernization debate. Programs designed to change the "culture" of poverty in which so many African Americans lived were put into effect, most notably with Johnson's Great Society. New national efforts in the fields of education, health care, job training, and civil and voting rights came into being. Significantly, the Johnson administration announced a "war on poverty," not a war on racism.

Almost immediately, however, another war reopened and illuminated the deep racial divisions in America and the ways in which those divisions were reflected in the nation's foreign policy. From the very beginning of the war in Vietnam, African Americans raised disquieting criticisms. Some suggested that African Americans were dying in disproportionate numbers in the conflict in Southeast Asia—and the numbers bore this out. In 1965 blacks accounted for nearly 25 percent of all U.S. combat deaths in Vietnam, though they made up approximately 11 percent of the total U.S. population. Outcries from the African American community soon got the attention of the American government, and some efforts were made to address the issue. Nevertheless, by 1968 blacks still made up over 13 percent of American fatalities in Vietnam.[19]

The reasons for this seem clear. Few African Americans served on draft boards, and in many Deep South states there were no African Americans on the local boards. The draft during the Vietnam War consistently struck hardest at the lowest socioeconomic levels of American society, hitting the black community with particular vigor. African Americans (and poor whites, for that matter) could not avail themselves of the numerous deferments that were heavily weighted toward the wealthy and white middle class. When it became apparent that a large percentage of African Americans—most of them products of a Jim Crow education system that was "separate" but hardly "equal" despite the 1954 Supreme Court school desegregation ruling in *Brown v. Topeka Board of Education*— could not pass the intelligence tests for induction into the military, the U.S. government merely lowered the standards with the "Project 100,000" program beginning in 1966. Once in the service, African Americans were disproportionately assigned to combat units. This is an especially dramatic turn of events given that in conflicts from the Civil War through World War II many U.S. policymakers and military leaders were skeptical about the fighting prowess of black troops. Statistics also revealed that black soldiers made up over half of the less-than-honorable discharges received by U.S. service personnel in Vietnam. Black soldiers made up 90 percent of the inmates of the infamous Long Binh Jail in Vietnam, and in August 1968, just months after the assassination of Martin Luther King Jr. and during the terrible 1968 race riots in America, the Long Binh prisoners rose up, engulfing the compound in violence and destruction for several days.

While initially supportive of President Johnson, who had been responsible for pushing through the 1964 Civil Rights Act and 1965 Voting Rights Act, African-American opinion on the war became decidedly

Selection from Vietnam, *a comic book written by Julian Bond and illustrated by T. G. Lewis. The publication came out shortly after Bond was expelled from the Georgia House of Representatives because of his opposition to the Vietnam War. He had expressed the outrage and anger felt by many African Americans concerning the war in Vietnam. As the first three panels make clear, black Americans were quick to see the connections between the war in Vietnam and the battle for civil rights at home. Source: Julian Bond,* Vietnam *(1967), illus. by T. G. Lewis, http://lists.village.virginia.edu/HTML_docs/Exhibits/Bond/Bond.html.*

negative much earlier and to a larger extent than white Americans' opinion did. A late-1967 poll showed that a much higher percentage of African Americans wanted to "get out quick." By 1969 over half of those blacks polled felt that the war was "immoral," while barely a third of whites felt the same way. Famous African Americans opposed the war, none in more dramatic fashion than the world heavyweight champion Muhammad Ali. Ali originally failed the intelligence test for service in the military, but when standards were lowered, he was called into the military. He refused, stating, "I ain't got nothing against them Viet Congs." He would not, he declared, "help continue the domination of white slavemasters over the darker people the world over." For his stand, Ali was stripped of his boxing title, was virtually banned from boxing, and was eventually tried and convicted for refusing induction. His conviction was later overturned.

Martin Luther King Jr.'s development into an antiwar activist perhaps best illuminates how race and the Vietnam War became hopelessly entangled. Like many other civil rights leaders, King became concerned when the United States involved itself in the war in Vietnam. His well-known views on nonviolence, sympathy for the poor and downtrodden, and deepening suspicions that the conflict would siphon President Johnson's attention and resources away from his Great Society programs all worked to create grave doubts in King's mind. However, as with many of his peers, he hesitated to criticize the war for fear of alienating Johnson and losing his support for the civil rights movement.

Finally, in February 1967, nearly two years after U.S. combat troops entered South Vietnam, King gave his first public speech against the war. Two months later, speaking at Riverside Church in New York, King charged that America had become "the greatest purveyor of violence in the world today." The nation should support people's revolutions, not oppose them, he stated, and urged his fellow countrymen to "admit that we have been wrong from the beginning" and "atone for our sins and errors" by removing our troops from Vietnam. And then King drew the direct connection he saw between racism at home and war abroad:

> Perhaps the more tragic recognition of reality took place when it became clear to me that the war was doing far more than devastating the hopes of the poor at home. It was sending their sons and their brothers and their husbands to fight and to die in extraordinarily high proportions relative to the rest of the population. We were taking the black young men who had been crippled by our society and sending them eight

thousand miles away to guarantee liberties in Southeast Asia which they had not found in southwest Georgia and East Harlem. So we have been repeatedly faced with the cruel irony of watching Negro and white boys on TV screens as they kill and die together for a nation that has been unable to seat them together in the same schools. So we watch them in brutal solidarity burning the huts of a poor village, but we realize that they would never live on the same block in Detroit. I could not be silent in the face of such cruel manipulation of the poor.[20]

The reaction from the Johnson administration was predictable. King instantly became persona non grata at the White House, and the FBI ratcheted up its investigations of the civil rights (and now antiwar) leader. A year later King was shot down by an assassin, and the nation's inner cities erupted into race riots. On their televisions, Americans were treated to an ironic spectacle during the newscasts in the summer of 1968. From Vietnam came footage of U.S. soldiers in the field, many of them African-American, attacking enemy strongholds while villages burned in the background. From Detroit and Washington, D.C., came footage of U.S. soldiers on the streets moving against rioters, all of them African-American, while cars and buildings burned in the background. Racism and U.S. foreign policy, which had been entangled since the nation's beginning, had become almost indistinguishable from one another.

CONCLUSION

IN THE WAKE OF THE DEVASTATING terrorist attacks on the United States on September 11, 2001, Americans were told again and again that the world had changed forever, that nothing would ever be the same, that their country now faced an unprecedented challenge. As the years have gone by, however, it seems that those observations might have been somewhat hasty. For most Americans, life has changed very little since 9/11. Aside from the thousands of U.S. troops who were sent to fight in Afghanistan and Iraq and their worried relatives, the "war on terrorism" has not brought about any noticeable upheavals in our society. Beyond the occasional references to orange, amber, and red alerts (colors creep into the jargon once again) and sometimes irritatingly long waits to get through airport security, the present conflict seems to have done little or nothing to change the daily lives of the vast majority of Americans.

There has, however, been one change that is most pertinent to the present study. Since 9/11 Americans have focused their attention on the Middle East as never before. Prior to the terrorist attacks the region had been defined, for the United States, by Israel and oil. The events of 2001 have certainly altered that definition. Israel and oil still command attention, to be sure, and still largely influence U.S. policy in the region. But, the war on terrorism has, really for the first time, brought Americans face to face with the nations—and the people—of the Middle East. What role, if any, will race play in this confrontation?

During the nineteenth and early twentieth centuries American views of the Middle East and the people who lived there were largely predicated on the religious historical meaning of the region. The Holy Land was a fascinating subject, and the Middle East came to be seen as the birthplace of Christianity. During the late 1800s the U.S. reading public

99

snatched up numerous novels describing the exotic (and often erotic) land of Arabia. In addition, American middle- and upper-class homes were cluttered with objects representing the mysterious Near East. As such, it became a favorite destination for American travelers who wanted to see the majesty and feel the spiritual power of Jerusalem and other sites mentioned in the Bible. As historian Melani McAlister explains, reading about the Holy Land was one thing, but actually visiting it and seeing the people who inhabited the area generally proved disappointing to the American traveler. Confronted with—and disappointed by—the non-Christian population they encountered, the Americans simply took this as "proof of the superiority of Christianity, since the failures of the local population to live up to the biblically inspired romantic hopes of Americans were generally explained as evidence of a general 'regression and decrepitude' that was connected both to the 'weaknesses and vices of the Ottoman rule' and to 'elements of the Mussulman character.'"[1]

And so into the early 1900s the American view of the Middle East and its people languished between disinterest and revulsion. The vacuum created by little scholarly work on the area and only scant direct contact between Americans and Middle Easterners was nicely filled by a dizzying variety of stereotypes. The region was alternatively quaint and backward, enticing and threatening, mysterious and deadly. Arab men became a wild mixture of dashing bandits and somewhat effeminate cowards, great lovers and vicious rapists. The women, as was often the case when Americans considered females in "primitive" regions, were generally seen as enticing enchantresses who usually led even strong-willed white, Christian men to their doom. All Arabs were sheikhs, everyone rode camels, and they spent most of their time wandering aimlessly from oasis to oasis. For its part, the U.S. government was largely content to leave the area to the British and French.

World War II dramatically increased the American interest in the Middle East, not as a place in and of itself but as a symbol of U.S. power and as a battleground in the Cold War. The immense oil reserves of the area and the establishment of the state of Israel in the postwar years now invested the Middle East with new meanings for the United States. In terms of understanding the people of the Middle East, however, old stereotypes were simply modified to fit the new reality. Nomadic, camel-riding sheikhs were now transformed into sunglass-wearing, greedy, smirking oil sheikhs, speeding by their oil fields in their Rolls-Royces. (Always with the implication, of course, that American engineers and technicians kept those oil wells pumping while the Arab sheikhs luxuriated with their harems and hookah pipes.) The romantic warriors of the tales of the Arabian nights and Lawrence of Arabia were now the vicious terrorists attacking the people of Israel.

Still, in the heady days of modernization theory following World War II, it still seemed possible to save the Middle East from itself. Michael Latham, quoting heavily from the popular sociologist David Lerner's 1958 study of "traditional society," summarizes the impact American society could have on these backward lands. "Driven by contact with the West, the modernization of the Middle East would penetrate all sectors of society and fundamentally change their structure." Industrialization and urbanization would appear. "In contrast with the isolated traditional society of the agricultural village, this new culture would carry with it a growing participatory ethos on which the foundations for political democracy could be built. Modernization, Lerner proclaimed, was irresistible. Even in the tradition-bound Middle East it represented 'the infusion of a rationalist and positivistic spirit against which, scholars seem agreed, Islam is defenseless.'"[2]

As the conflict in the Middle East intensified and spread beyond the borders of the region with highly publicized airplane hijackings and the murderous mayhem at the 1972 Munich Olympics, so too did the American perception of Arabs as a very different and now dangerous people. The seizure of the U.S. embassy in Tehran in 1979 by Muslim "fanatics" also had a bracing effect on American views of the "Arab" population. By the time of the first war with Iraq in 1991, an entirely new perception on how best to deal with these terrorists came into being. Edward Said explains:

> For at least a decade movies about American commandos pitted a hulking Rambo or technically whiz-like Delta Force against Arab/Muslim terrorist-desperadoes; in 1991 it was as if an almost metaphysical intention to rout Iraq had sprung into being, not because Iraq's offense, though great, was cataclysmic, but because a small non-white country had disturbed or rankled a suddenly energized super-nation imbued with a fervor that could only be satisfied with compliance or subservience from "sheikhs," dictators, and camel-jockeys. The truly acceptable Arabs would be those who like Anwar Sadat seemed purified almost completely of their bothersome national selfhood and might become folksy talk-show guests.[3]

By the twenty-first century a new stereotype of the Middle East was already taking shape, but the events of 9/11 cemented it into the

American mind. According to McAlister, "As the discourse of terrorist threat developed, during the Iran crisis and after, it helped to construct a subtle but crucial change in the imagined geography of the Middle East, a change that was marked by a reclassification: 'Islam' became highlighted as the dominant signifier of the region, rather than oil wealth, Arabs, or Christian Holy Lands." In addition, Islam "became conflated with 'terrorism.'" In just a short time the Middle East, which "had been understood, albeit incorrectly, as the 'Arab world' in the 1960s and 1970s became, again, incorrectly, 'the Islamic world' in the 1980s."[4] By the time the hijacked passenger jets plowed into the World Trade Center and the Pentagon in September 2001, it was a given that the "Islamic world" was also the center of world terrorism.

Once the attacks took place, racism against the people of the Middle East flared up dramatically. The FBI reported that hate crimes against Muslims and people of Middle Eastern descent increased by nearly 1,500 percent after the terrorist attacks. Arab Americans were detained at airport security and removed from planes, Islamic schools and mosques were vandalized, and at least two hate crime murders were committed. Hundreds of Arab Americans were arrested and thousands more were brought in for questioning by federal authorities. Peter Kirsanow, a Bush appointee to the U.S. Commission on Civil Rights, stated that if another terrorist attack was carried out by "a certain ethnic community or [people of] certain ethnicities . . . you can forget civil rights in this country." He went on to suggest that internment camps, such as those used to imprison Japanese Americans during World War II, might be necessary.[5]

And the power of racism can once again be seen in the Department of State, where Arab Americans are likely to find as cool a reception as that accorded to African Americans in decades past. Even before 9/11 Arab-American groups decried the lack of representation of their peers in the Department of State and other foreign policy offices and agencies. In 1998, for example, exactly one Arab American was serving in the State Department's Bureau of Near Eastern Affairs (responsible for the Middle East). He quickly drew criticism from Jewish-American groups and resigned after only a short time, claiming that individuals within the department wanted to "impose a rigid ideological litmus test on foreign service and exclude Arabs." Questions of "loyalty" continue to dog Arab Americans seeking a greater voice in America's foreign relations and a scarce few find their way into positions of importance in the Department of State.[6]

At first glance, nonhistorians may think it inconceivable that race continues to play a role in U.S. foreign policy. As a society we have made such great strides in race relations during the 230 years since the Declaration of Independence said that all men were created equal. Slavery has ended and civil rights have been granted to all American citizens regardless of color. Yet, when a historian looks at that same number of years, they see the blink of an eye. We recall that it was less than two hundred years ago that Samuel George Morton was filling his skulls with birdseed, that George Gliddon toured the country with his mummies, and that Thomas Jefferson worked out his algebraic calculations to determine what constituted a mulatto. A mere 160 years ago the United States provoked a war with Mexico to "liberate" certain lands from the control of a "mongrel" people. Just over one hundred years ago the United States embarked on its period of overseas expansion, battering its way into Cuba and the Philippines in order to carry the white man's burden. Barely one hundred years have passed since millions of Americans toured the grounds of the Louisiana Exposition, viewing the progress of the Anglo-Saxon race from barbarian to the most civilized people on earth and shaking their heads in wonder and revulsion at the Filipino natives who still seemed wedded to the Stone Age. Just over sixty years ago, racial animosities helped to create a "war without mercy" in the Pacific, during which thousands of Japanese Americans were placed in concentration camps in America. In the last forty years racism helped to lay the foundation for U.S. policy toward the apartheid regime in South Africa, define our enemy and our policies in the Vietnam War, and stereotype the people of the Middle East as "Islamic terrorists."

The longevity of racism, particularly in terms of its role in U.S. foreign policy, is not difficult to understand. Throughout the years, racism has demonstrated remarkable adaptability to the needs of American diplomacy, incredible resiliency in the face of challenges, and undeniable power which, on occasion, has actually overridden the needs of U.S. foreign policy. The use of a few examples from America's past should suffice to prove these points.

Racism has never been a static element in American foreign policy. Instead, it has shown a truly amazing ability to adapt to the specific needs of U.S. diplomacy at different times in the nation's history. During the days of Manifest Destiny, racism quickly came to the aid of the arguments for territorial expansion. It seemed perfectly natural, indeed inevitable, that the white race would overrun and displace the weaker races. In this particular instance, the weaker race was the "mongrel" mixture of the Mexicans, and most Americans expressed little doubt (and less sympathy) when it came to the question of seizing Texas, the New Mexico territory, and California. The Mexicans—backward, lazy, stupid, and completely incapable of self-improvement—simply had to give way to the march of progress. It was, after all, the destiny of the Anglo-Saxon race.

Half a century later Americans were once again bent on expansion. This time, however, the goal was markets not territory. And now the people in these faraway lands were not to be displaced or annihilated, for they would provide both labor to extract the mineral and agricultural wealth demanded by the American market and consumers for American products. American racial thought, now in the thrall of social Darwinism, again served as a bulwark for U.S. expansion, subtly adapting itself to the new demands of American diplomacy. Now the goal of U.S. policy was couched in terms of "uplift" and "civilization." It was painfully obvious that the peoples of Cuba, the Philippines, and other territories on which the American flag was planted were incapable of progress toward a civilized society if left to their own devices. They must be "freed" from the control of the inefficient (and racially suspect) Spaniards so that Yankee ingenuity could work its wonders on their primitive societies. The Louisiana Exposition made the point in dramatic fashion. At the Philippine Reservation visitors could see for themselves the choice before the American nation: leave the natives to their barbaric savagery or raise them to an acceptable level of civilization. Miraculously, this was also part of the destiny of the Anglo-Saxon race.

Racism has also proven itself nearly invulnerable to attacks from a variety of directions. Early in its development, for instance, the concept of race had to fend off challenges from religion. How could there be different races if God created man in his own image—and in one place? Such was the resilience of racial thinking, however, that it easily withstood these theological assaults. Racism turned the Bible against itself, arguing that the Tower of Babel story explained the diversity of mankind, that the dispersion of the human race to far-off corners of the world resulted in different kinds of people who had adapted to their new environments. Eventually, those who strongly supported racial theories simply dispensed with the pretense of monogenesis and argued that in contrast to the Biblical story of creation there had, in fact, been any number of creations. Early nineteenth-century science put the final nail in the coffin by "proving" the diversity of mankind; going further, they even suggested that the differences resulted in a hierarchy of races ranging from the strongest and most civilized (the Anglo-Saxon) to the weakest and most degraded (sometimes black, sometimes Native American).

Yet, when science turned against racism in the 1920s and 1930s with the new emphasis on culture instead of biology as an explanation for human differences and when the horrors of the Nazi regime signaled the death knell of scientific racism, racial thinking mutated once again. Like a virus, racism insinuated itself into the debates on culture and "modernization" in the 1950s and 1960s. The differences between Western society and "traditional" societies were no longer discussed in terms of skin color or cranial capacity but rather in terms of different cultural norms. Traditional societies just needed to be nudged into the "stages of economic growth." Much of this thinking, however, was racist thinking in sheep's clothing. Modernization theory still posited the same general thinking that lay behind American imperialism in the late nineteenth century: that traditional (i.e., nonwhite) societies were hopelessly and helplessly behind the modern (i.e., white) world. Only through the infusion of Western ideas into these cultures could they ever hope to move beyond their stagnant, backward status. In short, modernization depended on the acceptance of white leadership and the superiority of white culture. It was a rather remarkable feat. In the space of two hundred years, racism had beaten both religion and science to a standstill.

Finally, there is the undeniable power of racism. The purpose of this study has not been to suggest that race is the only determinant of U.S. foreign policy. But to deny race's role in American diplomacy is to have an incomplete understanding of the nature of America's international relations. And in some cases, the power of racism has been overwhelming—even when its power runs contrary to what would appear to be the goals of U.S. policy. Let us take but two examples. In 1919 the United States met with the other victorious Allied powers at Versailles to bring an official end to World War I and chart the future of the world. When Japan surprised many of the delegates by putting forward a resolution for international racial equality, the moment seemed propitious for the United States to rather easily gain the respect and possibly friendship of a growing power in the Far East. The resolution itself was rather innocuous and its application to the international scene was never spelled out in any specifics. The United States, therefore, seemed to have little to lose by supporting the resolution. Relations with the Japanese had always been somewhat tense, and it was undeniable that Japan had become a major player in the diplomatic jousting in Asia. President Woodrow Wilson, however, could not break free from the stranglehold of racism. His own personal views on the inferiority of other races, the powerful strains of racism running through his own nation, and the pressure applied by his Anglo-Saxon allies to thwart any attempt to introduce racial equality into the international arena led Wilson to squash the resolution even after it passed by an overwhelming majority.

Four decades later the United States confronted a strange turn of events. Its racism had been turned back upon it by communist propaganda that consistently homed in on racial injustices inside the "leader of the free world." America's "Achilles' heel," as the race problem was referred to, was steadily losing the nation prestige among both friends and foes. The U.S. commitment to the ideals it consistently professed—equality, justice, and democracy—suffered blow after blow as incidents of racism multiplied, highlighted by the ugly scenes coming out of Little Rock in 1957. The people of the world, particularly in Asia, Africa, and Latin America, were left to wonder whether America's rhetoric had any basis in reality. To confront this international public relations nightmare, the United States embarked on a truly novel approach to propaganda in 1958. America decided to admit to the world at the World's Fair in Brussels that it suffered from race problems, while at the same time suggesting that it was making progress in solving those problems and looked forward to the day when the United States would have a completely integrated society. It was a brave but ultimately futile gesture. The forces of racism in America immediately mounted a counterattack and found a receptive audience in President Dwight D. Eisenhower. Despite evidence that indicated that the "Unfinished Business" exhibit was having a positive impact on the world's perception of the United States, the American government first revised and then simply scrapped the section on segregation. Even in the heat of the Cold War, racism proved more powerful than national interest.

Given the history of racism in American foreign policy, what can we surmise about the future? The adaptability, resiliency, and power of racism suggest that we have not seen the end of its pernicious effects on the nation's international relations. Talk about the growing interdependence of nations and the increasing "smallness" of our world brought about by greater communication and transportation is not altogether comforting, for proximity and contact with other peoples has not often resulted in greater sympathy or understanding from Americans. Suggestions that diversity, multiculturalism, political correctness, and acceptance now dominate the intellectual climate of our nation are welcome, but racism has taken on challengers before and always come out on top. Efforts to increase Americans' knowledge of the world around them are laudable and altogether necessary. To argue that such knowledge in and of itself will lead to greater understanding and appreciation of other cultures only partially allays the fear that race will continue to impact America's relations with the world. Unless the United States is willing to forcefully and consistently come to grips with the role of race in its own society and come face to face with the damage that racism has left in its wake, it seems likely that race and racism will continue to haunt us at home and abroad. When questions are raised now and in the future about the nation's policies toward Africa, the Middle East, Asia, or Latin America, the strength and character of the United States demands that the answer, "I guess that's just the way things are around here," will no longer suffice.

APPENDIX OF
DOCUMENTS

White

1. BENJAMIN FRANKLIN, "OBSERVATIONS CONCERNING THE INCREASE OF MANKIND," 1751

Source: Leonard W. Labaree and William B. Wilcox, eds. The Papers of Benjamin Franklin *(New Haven: Yale University Press, 1959), 4:234.*

23. In fine, A Nation well regulated is like a Polypus; take away a Limb, its Place is soon supply'd; cut it in two, and each deficient Part shall speedily grow out of the Part remaining. Thus if you have Room and Subsistence enough, as you may by dividing, make ten Polypes out of one, you may of one make ten Nations, equally populous and powerful; rather, increase a Nation ten fold in Numbers and Strength.

And since Detachments of English from Britain sent to America, will have their Places at Home so soon supply'd and increase so largely here; why should the Palatine Boors [Germans] be suffered to swarm into our Settlements, and by herding together establish their Language and Manners to the Exclusion of ours? Why should Pennsylvania, founded by the English, become a Colony of Aliens, who will shortly be so numerous as to Germanize us instead of our Anglifying them, and will never adopt our Language or Customs, any more than they can acquire our Complexion.

24. Which leads me to add one Remark: That the Number of purely white People in the World is proportionably very small. All Africa is black

or tawny. Asia chiefly tawny. America (exclusive of the new Comers) wholly so. And in Europe, the Spaniards, Italians, French, Russians and Swedes, are generally of what we call a swarthy Complexion; as are the Germans also, the Saxons only excepted, who with the English, make the principal Body of White People on the Face of the Earth. I could wish their Numbers were increased. And while we are, as I may call it, Scouring our Planet, by clearing America of Woods, and so making this Side of our Globe reflect a brighter Light to the Eyes of Inhabitants in Mars or Venus, why should we in the Sight of Superior Beings, darken its People? Why increase the Sons of Africa, by Planting them in America, where we have so fair an Opportunity, by excluding all Blacks and Tawneys, of increasing the lovely White and Red? But perhaps I am partial to the Complexion of my Country, for such Kind of Partiality is natural to Mankind.

2. THOMAS JEFFERSON REFLECTS ON THE ISSUES OF AFRICAN AMERICANS AND SLAVERY, 1785

Source: Thomas Jefferson, "Notes on Virginia, Excerpts From Query XIV, 1785," in Thomas Jefferson: Revolutionary Philosopher: A Selection of Writings, *eds. John S. Pancake and N. Sharon Summers (Woodbury, NY: Barron's Educational Series, Inc., 1976), 309–316.*

Deep rooted prejudices entertained by the whites; ten thousand recollections, by the blacks, of the injuries they have sustained; new provocations; the real distinctions which nature has made; and many other circumstances, will divide us into parties, and produce convulsions which will probably never end but in the extermination of the one or the other race.—To these objections, which are political, may be added others, which are physical and moral. The first difference which strikes us is that of colour. Whether the black of the negro resides in the reticular membrane between the skin and scarf-skin, or in the scarf-skin itself; whether it proceeds from the colour of the blood, the colour of the bile, or from that of some other secretion, the difference is fixed in nature, and is as real as if its seat and cause were better known to us. And is this difference of no importance? Is it not the foundation of a greater or less share of beauty in the two races? Are not the fine mixtures of red and white, the expressions of every passion by greater or less suffusions of colour in the one, preferable to that eternal monotony, which reigns in the countenances, that immoveable veil of black which covers all the emotions of the other race? Add to these, flowing hair, a more elegant symmetry of form, their own judgment in favour of the whites, declared by their preference of them, as uniformly as is the preference of the Oranootan for the black women over those of his own species. The circumstance of superior beauty, is thought worthy attention in the propagation of our horses, dogs, and other domestic animals; why not in that of man? Besides those of colour, figure, and hair, there are other physical distinctions proving a difference of race. They have less hair on the face and body. They secrete less by the kidnies, and more by the glands of the skin, which gives them a very strong and disagreeable odour. This greater degree of transpiration renders them more tolerant of heat, and less so of cold, than the whites. Perhaps too a difference of structure in the pulmonary apparatus, which a late ingenious experimentalist has discovered to be the principal regulator of animal heat, may have disabled them from extricating, in the act of inspiration, so much of that fluid from the outer air, or obliged them in expiration, to part with more of it. They seem to require less sleep. A black, after hard labour through the day, will be induced by the slightest amusements to sit up till midnight, or later, though knowing he must be out with the first dawn of the morning. They are at least as brave, and more adventuresome. But this may perhaps proceed from a want of forethought, which prevents their seeing a danger till it be present. When present, they do not go through it with more coolness or steadiness than the whites. They are more ardent after their female: but love seems with them to be more an eager desire, than a tender delicate mixture of sentiment and sensation. Their griefs are transient. Those numberless afflictions, which render it doubtful whether heaven has given life to us in mercy or in wrath, are less felt, and sooner forgotten with them. In general, their existence appears to participate more of sensation than reflection. To this must be ascribed their disposition to sleep when abstracted from their diversions, and unemployed in labour. An animal whose body is at rest, and who does not reflect, must be disposed to sleep of course. Comparing them by their faculties of memory, reason, and imagination, it appears to me, that in memory they are equal to the whites; in reason much inferior, as I think one could scarcely be found capable of tracing and comprehending the investigations of Euclid; and that in imagination they are dull, tasteless, and anomalous. It would be unfair to follow them to Africa for this investigation. We will consider them here, on the same stage with the whites, and where the facts are not apocryphal on which a judgment is to be formed. It will be right to make great allowances for the difference of condition, of education, of conversation, of the sphere in which they move. Many millions of them have been brought to, and born in America. Most of them indeed have been confined to tillage, to their own homes, and their own society: yet many have been so situated, that they might have availed themselves of the conversation of their masters; many have been brought up to the handicraft arts, and from that circumstance have always been associated with the whites. Some have been liberally educated, and all have lived in countries where the arts and sciences are cultivated to a considerable degree, and have had before their eyes samples of the best works from abroad. But never yet could I find that a black had uttered a thought above the level of plain narration; never see even an elementary trait of painting or sculpture. The improvement of the blacks in body and mind, in the first instance of their mixture with the whites, has been observed by every one, and proves that their inferiority is not the effect merely of their condition of life. We know that among the Romans, about the Augustan age especially, the condition of their slaves was much more deplorable than that of the blacks on the continent of America.

But the slaves of which Homer speaks were whites. Notwithstanding these considerations which must weaken their respect for the laws of property, we find among them numerous instances of the most rigid integrity, and as many as among their better instructed masters, of benevolence, gratitude, and unshaken fidelity.—The opinion, that they are inferior in the faculties of reason and imagination, must be hazarded with great diffidence. To justify a general conclusion, requires many observations, even where the subject may be submitted to the Anatomical knife, to Optical glasses, to analysis by fire, or by solvents. How much more then where it is a faculty, not a substance, we are examining; where it eludes the research of all the senses; where the conditions of its existence are various and variously combined; where the effects of those which are present or absent bid defiance to calculation; let me add too, as a circumstance of great tenderness, where our conclusion would degrade a whole race of men from the rank in the scale of beings which their Creator may perhaps have given them. To our reproach it must be said, that though for a century and a half we have had under our eyes the races of black and of red men, they have never yet been viewed by us as subjects of natural history. I advance it therefore as a suspicion only, that the blacks, whether originally a distinct race, or made distinct by time and circumstances, are inferior to the whites in the endowments both of body and mind. It is not against experience to suppose, that different species of the same genus, or varieties of the same species, may possess different qualifications. Will not a lover of natural history then, one who views the gradations in all the races of animals with the eye of philosophy, excuse an effort to keep those in the department of man as distinct as nature has formed them? This unfortunate difference of colour, and perhaps of faculty, is a powerful obstacle to the emancipation of these people. Many of their advocates, while they wish to vindicate the liberty of human nature, are anxious also to preserve its dignity and beauty. Some of these, embarrassed by the question "What further is to be done with them?" join themselves in opposition with those who are actuated by sordid avarice only. Among the Romans emancipation required but one effort. The slave, when made free, might mix with, without staining the blood of his master. But with us a second is necessary, unknown to history. When freed, he is to be removed beyond the reach of mixture.

3. JOSIAH C. NOTT SPEAKS ON THE NATURAL HISTORY OF MANKIND, 1850

Source: Josiah C. Nott, An Essay on the Natural History of Mankind, Viewed in Connection With Negro Slavery: Delivered Before the Southern Rights Association, 14th December, 1850 *(Mobile, AL: Dade, Thompson & Co. Printers, 1851).*

Let us now take a retrospect of the ground we have passed over, and present, in a condensed form, the conclusions which may be deduced:

1st. It is conceded on all hands, that the Negroes have existed, with their present physical types, for at least four thousand years; that there is no evidence that they have any where during this time achieved civilization; that they have always shown inferior intelligence, and occupied the lowest grade in the scale of nations; and that they have always been the slaves of petty princes in Africa, by whom, and their parents, they have been sold to slavery in foreign nations.

2d. There is no example on record, to prove that climate, or any combination of known external agencies, can change a White Race into Negroes, or *vice versa.* This opinion, as far as I know, (and few books on the subject have escaped me) is sustained by every naturalist of repute of the present day.

3d. Though often asserted, there is not an atom of proof in the world's history, to show that a Race can be changed by cultivation, and raised in intelligence, from the lowest to the highest grade. The Negro, the Mongol, and Caucasian Races have maintained their relative grades, we *know,* from the Christian era to the present time, though all vicissitudes.

4th. From the past history of the Negroes, not a single fact or argument can be drawn to encourage the belief that the slaves of the United States can be colonized in Africa, or elsewhere, with a prospect of improving their condition; while there is ample reason to believe that it would bring incalculable evils upon them.

5th. That the slaves now in our Southern States must continue, with all their increase, to exist here as slaves, or be driven off to die of want and misery elsewhere.

Brown

4. PRESIDENT ANDREW JACKSON CALLS FOR THE REMOVAL OF NATIVE AMERICANS WESTWARD, 1830

Source: Andrew Jackson, "Second Annual Message," December 6, 1830, in James D. Richardson, A Compilation of the Messages and Papers of the Presidents 1789–1897, *vol. 2, 1817–1833 (Washington, D.C.: Government Printing Office, 1896), 519–23.*

It gives me great pleasure to announce to Congress that the benevolent policy of Government, steadily pursued for nearly thirty years, in relation to the removal of the Indians beyond the white settlements is approaching to a happy consummation. Two important tribes have accepted the provision made for their removal at the last session of Congress, and it is believed that their example will induce the remaining tribes also to seek the same obvious advantages.

The consequences of a speedy removal will be important to the United States, to individual States, and to the Indians themselves. The pecuniary advantages which it promises to the Government are the least of its recommendations. It puts an end to all possible danger of collision between the authorities of the General and State Governments on account of the Indians. It will place a dense and civilized population in large tracts of country now occupied by a few savage hunters. . . . It will separate the Indians from immediate contact with settlements of whites; free them from the power of the States; enable them to pursue happiness in their own way and under their own rude institutions; will retard the progress of decay, which is lessening their numbers, and perhaps cause them gradually, under the protection of the Government and through the influence of good counsels, to cast off their savage habits and become an interesting, civilized, and Christian community.

Toward the aborigines of the country no one can indulge a more friendly feeling than myself, or would go further in attempting to reclaim them from their wandering habits and make them a happy, prosperous people.

Humanity has often wept over the fate of the aborigines of this country, and philanthropy has been long busily employed in devising means to avert it, but its progress has never for a moment been arrested, and one by one have many powerful tribes disappeared from the earth. To follow to the tomb the last of his race and to tread on the graves of extinct nations excite melancholy reflections. But true philanthropy reconciles the mind to these vicissitudes as it does to the extinction of one generation to make room for another. In the monuments and fortresses of an unknown people, spread over the extensive regions of the West, we behold the memorials of a once powerful race, which was exterminated or has disappeared to make room for the existing savage tribes. Nor is there anything in this which, upon a comprehensive view of the general interests of the human race, is to be regretted. Philanthropy could not wish to see this continent restored to the conditions in which it was found by our forefathers. What good man would prefer a country covered with forests and ranged by a few thousand savages to our extensive Republic, studded with cities, towns, and prosperous farms, embellished with all the improvements which art can devise or industry execute, occupied by more than 12,000,000 happy people, and filled with all the blessings of liberty, civilization, and religion?

The present policy of the Government is but a continuation of the same progressive change by a milder process. The tribes which occupied the countries now constituting the Eastern States were annihilated or have melted away to make room for the whites. The waves of population and civilization are rolling to the westward, and we now propose to acquire the countries occupied by the red men of the South and West by a fair exchange, and, at the expense of the United States, to send them to a land where their existence may be prolonged and perhaps made perpetual. Doubtless it will be painful to leave the graves of their fathers; but what do they more than our ancestors did or than our children are now doing? To better their condition in an unknown land our forefathers left all that was dear in earthly objects. Our children by thousands yearly leave the land of their birth to seek new homes in distant regions. Does Humanity weep at these painful separations from everything, animate and inanimate, with which the young heart has become entwined? Far from it. It is rather a source of joy that our country affords scope where our young population may range unconstrained in body or in mind, developing the power and faculties of man in their highest perfection. These remove hundreds and almost thousands of miles at their own expense, purchase the lands they occupy, and support themselves at their new homes from the moment of their arrival. Can it be cruel in this Government when, by events which it can not control, the Indian is made discontented in his ancient home to purchase his lands, to give him a new and extensive territory, to pay the expense of his removal, and support him a year in his new abode? How many thousands of our own people would gladly embrace the opportunity of removing to the West on such conditions! If the offers made to the Indians were extended to them, they would be hailed with gratitude and joy.

And is it supposed that the wandering savage has a stronger attachment to his home than the settled, civilized Christian? Is it more afflicting to him to leave the graves of his fathers than it is to our brothers and children? Rightly considered, the policy of the General Government toward the red man is not only liberal, but generous. He is unwilling to submit to the laws of the States and mingle with their population. To save him from this alternative, or perhaps utter annihilation, the General Government kindly offers him a new home, and proposes to pay the whole expense of his removal and settlement.

May we not hope, therefore, that all good citizens, and none more zealously than those who think the Indians oppressed by subjection to the laws of the States, will unite in attempting to open the eyes of those children of the forest to their true condition, and by a speedy removal to relieve them from all the evils, real or imaginary, present or prospective, with which they may be supposed to be threatened.

5. SAM HOUSTON RALLIES HIS FELLOW TEXANS, 1836

Source: "Sam Houston to His Soldiers, January 15, 1836," in Constructing the American Past: A Source Book of a People's History, *eds. Elliott J. Gorn, Randy Roberts, and Terry D. Bilhartz (New York: Pearson Longman, 2005), 1:175.*

. . . let us then, comrades, sever that link that binds us to that rusty chain of the Mexican Confederation; let us break off the live slab from the dying cactus that it may not dry up with the remainder; let us plant it anew that it may spring luxuriantly out of the fruitful savannah. Nor will the vigor of the descendents of the sturdy north ever mix with the phlegm of the indolent Mexicans, no matter how long we may live among them. Two different tribes on the same hunting ground will never get along together. The tomahawk will ever fly and the scalping knife will never rest until the last of either one tribe or the other is either destroyed or is a slave. And I ask, comrades, will we ever bend our necks as slaves, ever quietly watch the destruction of our property and the annihilation of our guaranteed rights? NO!! Never! Too well I know my people. The last drop of our blood would flow before we would bow under the yoke of these half-Indians.

6. JOHN FISKE ON THE EVOLUTION OF RACES, 1873

Source: John Fiske, "The Progress From Brute to Man," North American Review 241 (October 1873): 255–256.

In similar wise is made to disappear the sharp contrast between human and brute animals in capability of progress. Hardly any fact is more imposing to the imagination than the fact that each generation of men is perceptibly more enlightened than the preceding one, while each generation of brutes exactly resembles those which have come before it. But the contrast is obtained only by comparing the civilized European of today directly with the brute animals known to us through the short period of recorded human history. The capability of progress, however, is by no means shared alike by all races of men. Of the numerous races historically known to us, it has been manifested in a marked degree only by two,—the Aryan and Semitic. To a much less conspicuous extent it has been exhibited by the Chinese and Japanese, the Copts of Egypt, and a few of the highest American races. On the other hand, the small-brained races—the Australians and Papuans, the Hottentots, and the majority of tribes constituting the wide-spread Malay and American families—appear almost wholly incapable of progress, even under the guidance of higher races. The most that can be said for them is, that they are somewhat more imitative and somewhat more teachable than any brute animals. In the presence of the Aryan, even under the most favorable circumstances, they tend to become extinguished, rather than to appropriate the results of a civilization which there is no reason to suppose they could ever have originated. The two great races of Middle Africa, the Negroes and Kaffirs, have shown, by their ability to endure slave labor, their superiority to those above mentioned; but their career, where it has not been interfered with by white men, has been but little less monotonous than the career of a brute species. Of all these barbarian races, we commonly say that they have no history; and by this we mean that throughout long ages they have made no appreciable progress. In a similar sense we should say of a race of monkeys or elephants, that it has no history.

7. REVEREND JOSIAH STRONG PROPHESIZES ON GOD, THE ANGLO-SAXON, AND THE WORLD, 1891

Source: Josiah Strong, Our Country, *ed. Jurgen Herbst (Cambridge: Belknap Press of Harvard University Press, 1963), 213–218.*

It seems to me that God, with infinite wisdom and skill, is training the Anglo-Saxon race for an hour sure to come in the world's future. Heretofore there has always been in the history of the world a comparatively unoccupied land westward, into which the crowded countries of the East have poured their surplus populations. But the widening waves of migration, which millenniums ago rolled east and west from the valley of Euphrates, meet to-day on our Pacific coast. There are no more new worlds. The unoccupied arable lands of the earth are limited, and will soon be taken. The time is coming when the pressure of population on the means of subsistence will be felt here as it now felt in Europe and Asia. Then will the world enter upon a new stage of its history—*the final competition of races, for which the Anglo-Saxon is being schooled.* Long before the thousand millions are here, the mighty *centrifugal* tendency, inherent in this stock and strengthened in the United States, will assert itself. Then this race of unequaled energy, with all the majesty of numbers and the might of wealth behind it—the representative, let us hope, of the largest liberty, the purest Christianity, the highest civilization—having developed peculiarly aggressive traits calculated to impress its institutions upon mankind, will spread itself over the earth. If I read not amiss, this powerful race will move down upon Mexico, down upon Central and South America, out upon the islands of the sea, over upon Africa and beyond. And can anyone doubt that the result of this competition of the races will be the "survival of the fittest?"

. . . To this result no war of extermination is needful; the contest is not one of arms, but of vitality and of civilization. "At the present day," says Mr. Darwin, "civilized nations are everywhere supplanting barbarous nations, excepting where the climate opposes a deadly barrier; and they succeed mainly, though not exclusively, through their arts, which are the products of the intellect." Thus the Finns were supplanted by the Aryan races in Europe and Asia, the Tartars by the Russians, and thus the aborigines of North America, Australia and New Zealand are now disappearing before the all-conquering Anglo-Saxons. It seems as if these inferior tribes were only precursors of a superior race, voices in the wilderness crying: "Prepare ye the way of the Lord!"

Whether the extinction of the inferior races before the advancing Anglo-Saxon seems to the reader sad or otherwise, it certainly appears probable. I know of nothing except climatic conditions to prevent this race from populating Africa as it has peopled North America.

In my own mind, there is no doubt that the Anglo-Saxon is to exercise the commanding influence in the world's future; but the exact nature of that influence is, as yet, undetermined. How far his civilization will be materialistic and atheistic, and how long it will take thoroughly to Christianize and sweeten it, how rapidly he will hasten the coming of the kingdom wherein dwelleth righteousness, or how many ages he may retard it, is still uncertain; but *is now being swiftly determined.* Let us weld together in a chain the various links of our logic which we have endeavored to forge. Is it manifest that the Anglo-Saxon holds in his hands the destinies of mankind for ages to come? Is it evident that the United States is to be the home of this race, the principal seat of his power, the great center of his influence? Is it true that the great West is to dominate the nation's future? Has it been shown that this generation is to determine the character, and hence the destiny of the West?

Notwithstanding the great perils which threaten it, I cannot think our civilization will perish; but I believe it is fully in the hands of the Christians of the United States, during the next ten or fifteen years, to hasten or retard the coming of Christ's kingdom in the world by hundreds, and perhaps thousands, of years. We of this generation and nation occupy the Gibraltar of the ages which commands the world's future.

8. SENATOR ALBERT J. BEVERIDGE DEFENDS AMERICA'S ACTIONS IN THE PHILIPPINES, JANUARY 9, 1900

Source: U.S. Congress, Congressional Record*, 56th Cong., 1st sess., 33, 704–712.*

It has been charged that our conduct of the war has been cruel. . . . Senators must remember that we are not dealing with Americans or Europeans. We are dealing with Orientals. We are dealing with Orientals who are Malays. We are dealing with Malays instructed in Spanish methods. They mistake kindness for weakness, forbearance for fear. It could not be otherwise unless you could erase hundreds of years of savagery, other hundreds of years of Orientalism, and still other hundreds of years of Spanish character and custom.

. . . it would be better to abandon this combined garden and Gibraltar of the Pacific, and count our blood and treasure already spent a

profitable loss than to apply any academic arrangement of self-government to these children. They are not capable of self-government. How
could they be? They are not of a self-governing race. They are Orientals,
Malays, instructed by Spaniards in the latter's worst estate.

They know nothing of practical government except as they have
witnessed the weak, corrupt, cruel, and capricious rule of Spain. What
magic will anyone employ to dissolve in their minds and characters those
impressions of governors and governed which three centuries of misrule
has created? What alchemy will change the Oriental quality of their blood
and set the self-governing currents of the American pouring through
their Malay veins? How shall they, in the twinkling of an eye, be exalted to
the heights of self-governing peoples which required a thousand years of
rule for us to reach, Anglo-Saxons though we are?

Mr. President, this question is deeper than any question of party
politics; deeper than any question of the isolated policy of our country
even; deeper even than any question of constitutional power. It is el-
emental. It is racial. God has not been preparing the English-speaking
and Teutonic peoples for a thousand years for nothing but vain and idle
self-contemplation and self-admiration. No! He has made us the master
organizers of the world to establish system where chaos reigns. He has
given us the spirit of progress to overwhelm the forces of reaction throughout the earth. He has made us adepts in government that we may admin-
ister government among the savage and senile peoples. Were it not for
such a force as this the world would relapse into barbarism and night.
And of all our race He has marked the American people as His chosen
nation to finally lead in the regeneration of the world. This is the divine
mission of America, and it holds for us all the profit, all the glory, all the
happiness possible to man. We are trustees of the world's progress, guard-
ians of its righteous peace. The judgment of the Master is upon us: "Ye
have been faithful over a few things; I will make you ruler over many
things."

Yellow

9. ANTI-CHINESE SENTIMENT IN CALIFORNIA, 1878

*Source: Dennis Kearney and H. L. Knight, "Appeal From California: The Chinese Invasion:
Workingmen's Address," Indianapolis Times, February 28, 1878.*

Here, in San Francisco, the palace of the millionaire looms up above the
hovel of the starving poor with as wide a contrast as anywhere on earth.

To add to our misery and despair, a bloated aristocracy has sent to China— the greatest and oldest despotism in the world—for a cheap working slave. It rakes the slums of Asia to find the meanest slave on earth—the Chinese coolie—and imports him here to meet the free American in the Labor market, and still further widen the breach between the rich and the poor, still further to degrade white Labor. These cheap slaves fill every place. Their dress is scant and cheap. Their food is rice from China. They hedge twenty in a room, ten by ten. They are whipped curs, abject in docility, mean, contemptible and obedient in all things. They have no wives, children or dependents.

California must be all American or all Chinese. We are resolved that it shall be American, and are prepared to make it so. May we not rely upon your sympathy and assistance?

10. LOTHROP STODDARD WARNS OF THE RISING YELLOW TIDE, 1922

Source: Lothrop Stoddard, The Rising World of Color Against White World-Supremacy *(New York: Charles Scribner's Sons, 1922), 8–9, 48–49, 231–232.*

On the other hand, none of the colored races shows perceptible signs of declining birth-rate, all tending to breed up to the limits of available subsistence. . . .

Now what must be the inevitable result of all this? It can mean only one thing: a tremendous and steadily augmenting outward thrust of surplus colored men from overcrowded colored homelands. . . . Where, then, should the congested colored world tend to pour its accumulating human surplus, inexorably condemned to emigrate or starve? The answer is: into those emptier regions of the earth under white political control. But many of these relatively empty lands have been definitely set aside by the white man as his own special heritage. The up-shot is that the rising flood of color finds itself walled in by white dikes debarring it from many a promised land which it would fain deluge with its dusky waves.

Thus, for Japanese migration, neither the empty spaces of northern or southern Asia will do. The natural outlets lie outside Asia in the United States, Australasia, and the temperate parts of Latin America. . . . There lies a danger, not merely to the peace of the Far East, but to the peace of the world. Fired by a fervent patriotism; resolved to make their country a leader among the nations; the Japanese writhe at the constriction of their present race-bounds. . . . In short: Japan must find lands where Japanese can breed by the tens of millions if she is not to be automatically overshadowed in course of time, even assuming that she does not suffocate or blow up from congestion before that time arrives. This is the secret of her aggressive foreign policy, her chronic imperialism, her extravagant dreams of conquest and "world domination."

. . . In my opening chapters I discussed the rapid growth of Asiatic populations and the resultant steadily augmenting outward thrust of surplus Asiatics (principally yellow men, but also in lesser degree brown men) from overcrowded homelands toward the less-crowded regions of the earth. It is, in fact, Asiatics, and above all Mongolian Asiatics, who form the first wave of the rising tide of color. Unfortunately, the white world cannot permit this rising tide free scope. White men cannot, under peril of their very race-existence, allow wholesale Asiatic immigration into white race-areas. This prohibition, which will be discussed in the next chapter, is already a serious blow to Asiatic aspirations.

But the matter does not end there. The white world also cannot permit with safety to itself wholesale Asiatic penetration of non-Asiatic colored regions like black Africa and tropical Latin America. To permit Asiatic colonization and ultimate control of these vast territories with their incalculable resources would be to overturn in favor of Asia the political, the economic, and eventually the racial balance of power in the world. At present the white man controls these regions. And he must stand fast. No other course is possible. Neither black Africa nor mongrel-ruled tropical America can stand alone. If the white man goes, the Asiatic comes—browns to Africa, yellows to Latin America. And there is no reason under heaven why we whites should deliberately present Asia with the richest regions of the tropics, to our own impoverishment and probable undoing.

Our race-duty is therefore clear. We must resolutely oppose both Asiatic permeation of white race-areas and Asiatic inundation of those non-white, but equally non-Asiatic, regions inhabited by the really inferior races.

11. *TIME* INSTRUCTS ITS READERS ON HOW TO TELL A "JAP" FROM A "FRIEND," 1941

Source: "How to Tell Your Friends From the Japs," Time, December 22, 1941, 33.

Virtually all Japanese are short. Japanese are likely to be stockier and broader-hipped than short Chinese. Japanese are seldom fat; they often dry up and grow lean as they age. Although both have the typical epicanthic fold of the upper eyelid, Japanese eyes are usually set closer together. The Chinese expression is likely to be more placid, kindly, open; the Japanese more positive, dogmatic, arrogant. Japanese are hesitant, nervous in conversation, laugh loudly at the wrong time. Japanese walk stiffly erect, hard-heeled. Chinese, more relaxed, have an easy gait, sometimes shuffle.

12. CHARLES LINDBERGH WITNESSES THE WAR IN THE PACIFIC, 1944

Source: Charles A. Lindbergh, The Wartime Journals of Charles A. Lindbergh *(New York: Harcourt Brace Jovanovich, Inc., 1970), 879–880, 882–883, 903, 919, 923.*

Friday, June 21
    . . . sitting in the security and relative luxury of our quarters, I listen to American Army officers refer to these Japanese soldiers as "yellow sons of bitches." Their desire is to exterminate the Jap ruthlessly, even cruelly. I have not heard a word of respect or compassion spoken of our enemy since I came here.

    We must bomb them out, those Jap soldiers, because this is war, and if we do not kill them, they will kill us now that we have removed the possibility of surrender. But I would have more respect for the character of our people if we could give them a decent burial instead of kicking in the teeth of their corpses, and pushing their bodies into hollows in the ground, scooped out and covered up by bulldozers. After that, we will leave their graves unmarked and say, "That's the only way to handle the yellow sons of bitches."

Monday, July 24
    Going down the hill, we came to a pass with the bodies of a Japanese officer and ten or twelve soldiers lying sprawled about in the gruesome positions which only mangled bodies can take. . . . And as one of the officers with me said, "I see that the infantry have been up to their favorite occupation," i.e., knocking out all the teeth that contain gold fillings for souvenirs.

Saturday, September 9
    Before the [Japanese] bodies in the hollow were "bulldozed over," the officer said, a number of our Marines went in among them, searching through their pockets and prodding around in their mouths for gold-filled teeth. Some of the Marines, he said, had a little sack in which they collected teeth with gold fillings. The officer said he had seen a number of Japanese bodies from which an ear or a nose had been cut off. "Our

boys cut them off to show their friends in fun, or to dry and take back to the States when they go. We found one Marine with a Japanese head. He was trying to get the ants to clean the flesh off the skull, but the odor got so bad we had to take it away from him." It is the same everywhere I go. *Thursday, September 14*

Cleared customs and we drove out to the base. (The customs officer asked me if I had any bones in my baggage. He said they had to ask everyone that question because they had found a large number of men taking Japanese bones back home for souvenirs. He said he had found one man with two "green" Jap skulls in his baggage.)

Black

13. "CONSTRUCTIVE ENGAGEMENT" WITH WHITE REGIMES IN SOUTHERN AFRICA, 1969

Source: National Security Council Interdepartmental Group for Africa, "Study in Response to National Security Study Memorandum 39: Southern Africa," December 9, 1969, http://nsarchive.chadwyck.com/nsa/documents/SA/00379/all.pdf.

OPTION 2

Premise

The whites are here to stay and the only way that constructive change can come about is through them. There is no hope for the blacks to gain the political rights they seek through violence, which will only lead to chaos and increased opportunities for the communists. We can, by selective relaxation of our stance toward the white regimes, encourage some modification of their current racial and colonial policies and through more substantial economic assistance to the black states (a total of about $5 million annually in technical assistance to the black states) help to draw the two groups together and exert some influence on both for peaceful change. Our tangible interests form a basis for our contacts in the region, and these can be maintained at an acceptable political cost.

General Posture

We would maintain public opposition to racial repression but relax political isolation and economic restrictions on the white states. We would begin by modest indications of this relaxation, broadening the scope of our relations and contacts gradually and to some degree in response to tangible—albeit small and gradual—moderation of white policies. Without openly taking a position undermining the U.K. and the UN on Rhodesia, we would be more flexible in our attitude toward the Smith regime. We would take present Portuguese policies as suggesting further changes in the Portuguese Territories. At the same time we would take diplomatic steps to convince the black states of the area that their current liberation and majority rule aspirations in the south are not attainable by violence and that their only hope for a peaceful and prosperous future lies in closer relations with white-dominated states. . . .

This option accepts, at least over a 3 to 5 year period, the prospect of unrequited U.S. initiatives toward the whites and some opposition from the blacks in order to develop an atmosphere conducive to change in white attitudes through persuasion and erosion. To encourage this change in white attitudes, we would indicate our willingness to accept political arrangements short of guaranteed progress toward majority rule, provided that they assure broadened political participation in some form by the whole population.

THE U.S. AND THE AFRICAN STATES IN THE UNITED NATIONS

The main U.S. political interest in southern African issues at the UN is to keep these issues manageable. On the one hand, we seek to maintain a credible stance on racial questions in the eyes of the black African nations, while on the other we attempt to discourage the adoption of unrealistic measures which would damage other U.S. interests in the area and the UN itself.

14. U.S. GI TESTIFIES ABOUT ATROCITIES AND "GOOKS," 1971

Source: Vietnam Veterans Against the War, The Winter Soldier Investigation: An Inquiry Into American War Crimes *(Boston: Beacon Press, 1972), 43–45.*

Sgt. Jamie Henry, 4th Infantry Division
On August 8th our company executed a 10-year-old boy. We shot him in the back with a full magazine M-16. Approximately August 16th to August 20th—I'm not sure of the date—a man was taken out of his hootch sleeping, was put into a cave, and he was used for target practice by a lieutenant, the same lieutenant who had ordered the boy killed. Now they used him for target practice with an M-60, an M-16, and a 45.

I don't want to go into the details of these executions because the executions are a direct result of a policy. It's the policy that is important. The executions are secondary because the executions are created by the policy that is, I believe, a conscious policy within the military. Number one, the racism in the military is so rampant. Now you have all heard of the military racism. It's institutionalized; it is policy; it is SOP [standard operating procedure]; you are trained to be a racist. When you go into basic training, you are taught that the Vietnamese are not people. You are taught they are gooks and all you hear is "gook, gook, gook, gook." And once you take the Vietnamese people, or any of the Asian people, because the Asian serviceman in Vietnam is the brunt of the same racism because the GIs over there do not distinguish one Asian from another. They are trained so thoroughly that all Asians become the brunt of this racism.

You are trained "gook, gook, gook," and once the military has got the idea implanted in your mind that these people are not humans, they are subhuman, it makes it a little bit easier to kill 'em. One barrier is removed, and this is intentional, because obviously, the purpose of the military is to kill people. And if you're not an effective killer, they don't want you. The military doesn't distinguish between North Vietnamese, South Vietnamese, Viet Cong, civilian—all of them are gooks, all of them are considered to be subhuman. None of them are any good, etc. And all of them can be killed and most of them are killed.

15. MARTIN LUTHER KING JR. CONDEMNS THE VIETNAM WAR, 1967

Source: Martin Luther King Jr., "The Casualties of the War in Vietnam" (speech, Los Angeles, CA, February 25, 1967), http://www.stanford.edu/group/King/about_king/encyclopedia/vietnam.htm.

But honesty impels me to admit that our power has often made us arrogant. We feel that our money can do anything. We arrogantly feel that we have everything to teach other nations and nothing to learn from them. We often arrogantly feel that we have some divine, messianic mission to police the whole world. We are arrogant in not allowing young nations to go through the same growing pains, turbulence and revolution that characterized our history. We are arrogant in our contention that we have some sacred mission to protect people from totalitarian rule, while we make little use of our power to end the evils of South Africa and Rhodesia, and while we are in fact supporting dictatorships with guns and money under the guise of fighting Communism. We are arrogant in professing to be concerned about the freedom of foreign nations while not setting our own house in order. Many of our Senators and Congressmen vote joyously to appropriate billions of dollars for war in Viet Nam, and these same Senators and Congressmen vote loudly against a Fair Housing Bill to make it possible for a Negro veteran of Viet Nam to purchase a decent home. We arm Negro soldiers to kill on foreign battlefields, but offer little protection for their relatives from beatings and killings in our own south. We are willing to make the Negro 100% of a citizen in warfare, but reduce him to 50% of a citizen on American soil. Of all the good things in life the Negro has approximately one half those of whites; of the bad he has twice that of whites. Thus, half of all Negroes live in substandard housing and Negroes have half the income of whites. When we turn to the negative experiences of life, the Negro has a double share. There are twice as many unemployed. The infant mortality rate is double that of whites. There are twice as many Negroes in combat in Viet Nam at the beginning of 1967 and twice as many died in action (20.6%) in proportion to their numbers in the population as whites. All of this reveals that our nation has not yet used its vast resources of power to end the long night of poverty, racism and man's inhumanity to man.

Source: Martin Luther King Jr., "Beyond Vietnam: A Time to Break Silence" (speech, Riverside Church, New York, April 4, 1967), http://www.hartford-hwp.com/archives/45a/058.html.

Perhaps the more tragic recognition of reality took place when it became clear to me that the war was doing far more than devastating the hopes of the poor at home. It was sending their sons and their brothers and their husbands to fight and to die in extraordinarily high proportions relative to the rest of the population. We were taking the black young men who had been crippled by our society and sending them eight thousand miles away to guarantee liberties in Southeast Asia which they had not found in southwest Georgia and East Harlem. So we have been repeatedly faced with the cruel irony of watching Negro and white boys on TV screens as they kill and die together for a nation that has been unable to seat them together in the same schools. So we watch them in brutal solidarity burning the huts of a poor village, but we realize that they would never live on the same block in Detroit. I could not be silent in the face of such cruel manipulation of the poor.

NOTES

Chapter 1: White

1. Thomas Jefferson, letter to Francis C. Gray, March 4, 1815, in *The Complete Jefferson: Containing His Major Writings Published and Unpublished, Except His Letters*, ed. Saul K. Padover (Freeport, NY: Books for Libraries Press, 1969), 1022–23.
2. Thomas F. Gossett, *Race: The History of an Idea in America* (Dallas: Southern Methodist University Press, 1963), 19.
3. Michael H. Hunt, *Ideology and U.S. Foreign Policy* (New Haven: Yale University Press, 1987), 46.
4. Gary B. Nash, "Red, White, and Black: The Origins of Racism in Colonial America," in *The Great Fear: Race in the Mind of America*, eds. Gary B. Nash and Richard Weiss (New York: Holt, Rinehart and Winston, 1970), 15.
5. Reginald Horsman, *Race and Manifest Destiny: The Origins of American Racial Anglo-Saxonism* (Cambridge: Harvard University Press, 1981), 24.

Chapter 2: Brown

1. Heather Pringle, *The Mummy Congress: Science, Obsession, and the Everlasting Dead* (New York: Hyperion, 2001), 182–83.
2. Andrew Jackson, "Second Annual Message," December 6, 1830, in James D. Richardson, *A Compilation of the Messages and Papers of the Presidents, 1789–1897*, vol. 2, *1817–1833* (Washington, D.C.: Government Printing Office, 1896), 519–23.
3. Houston quote found in Arnoldo de León, *They Called Them Greasers: Anglo Attitudes Toward Mexicans in Texas, 1821–1900* (Austin: University of Texas Press, 1983), 7; Austin quote found in David J. Weber, "'Scarce More Than Apes': Historical Roots of Anglo American Stereotypes of Mexicans in the Border Region," in *New Spain's Far*

Northern Frontier: Essays on Spain in the New West, 1540–1821 (Albuquerque: University of New Mexico Press, 1979), 92.

4. "Petition From the Committee of Vigilance and Public Safety for the Municipality of San Augustin, 1835," in *Constructing the American Past: A Source Book of a People's History*, 5th ed., eds. Elliott J. Gorn, Randy Roberts, and Terry D. Bilhartz (New York: Pearson Longman, 2005), 1:174.

5. For a compilation of newspaper editorials and speeches concerning the war with Mexico, see "U.S. 'Theft' of Mexican Territory," comp., Chris Schefler, http://academic.udayton.edu/race/02rights/guadalu3.htm (accessed May 8, 2006).

6. Quotes found in Horsman, *Race and Manifest Destiny*, 242.

7. Gossett, *Race*, 154.

8. John Fiske, "The Progress From Brute to Man," *North American Review* 241 (October 1873): 251–319.

9. Josiah Strong, *Our Country*, ed. Jurgen Herbst (Cambridge: Belknap Press of Harvard University Press, 1963), 214–16.

10. Gossett, *Race*, 315, 322; Alfred Thayer Mahan, *The Influence of Sea Power Upon History, 1660–1783* (Boston: Little, Brown and Company, 1890), 82; Alfred Thayer Mahan, letter to Samuel A. Ashe, March 11, 1885, *Letters and Papers of Alfred Thayer Mahan*, eds. Robert Seager II and Doris D. Maguire (Annapolis: Naval Institute Press, 1975), 1: 593.

11. Thomas G. Dyer, *Theodore Roosevelt and the Idea of Race* (Baton Rouge: Louisiana State University Press, 1980), 141, 147–49.

12. Strong, *Our Country*, 213–14.

13. "Albert J. Beveridge's Salute to Imperialism, 1900," in *Major Problems in American Foreign Relations*, Vol. 1, *To 1920*, 4th ed., eds. Thomas G. Paterson and Dennis Merrill (Lexington, MA: D. C. Heath, 1995), 424–26; Gossett, *Race*, 337.

14. John J. Johnson, *Latin America in Caricature* (Austin: University of Texas Press, 1980).

15. The other substantial Spanish colony taken in the war, Puerto Rico, was subjected to a different fate. Like the Cubans, the Puerto Ricans were found to be a decidedly inferior mixed race. As one social scientist put it in 1901, the various admixtures of blood on the island resulted in a "thin-blooded people." See Philip W. Kennedy, "Race and American Expansion in Cuba and Puerto Rico, 1985–1905," *Journal of Black Studies* 1 (1971): 306–16. Unlike Cuba and the Philippines, both of which were eventually granted independence, Puerto Rico found itself in a political limbo—its people were granted U.S. citizenship in 1917, but not full political rights. It was not until 1947 that Puerto Ricans were allowed to elect their own local officials.

Five years later the island was granted the status of a "common-wealth," which it remains to this day.

16. "William McKinley's Imperial Gospel, 1899," in *Major Problems*, 424.
17. Gossett, *Race*, 329.
18. Dyer, *Theodore Roosevelt*, 140.
19. James Bradley, *Flyboys: A True Story of Courage* (Boston: Little, Brown and Company, 2003), 70.

Chapter 3: Yellow

1. Sax Rohmer, *The Insidious Dr. Fu-Manchu* (Mineola, NY: Dover Publications, 1997), 13.
2. Stuart Creighton Miller, *The Unwelcome Immigrant: The American Image of the Chinese, 1785–1882* (Berkeley: University of California Press, 1969).
3. Stuart Creighton Miller, "The American Trader's Image of China, 1785–1840," *Pacific Historical Review* 36 (1967): 391.
4. Luther W. Spoehr, "Sambo and the Heathen Chinee: Californians' Racial Stereotypes in the Late 1870s," *Pacific Historical Review* 42 (1973): 190–91; Blaine quote is found in Gossett, *Race*, 291; P. W. Dooner, *Last Days of the Republic* (New York: Arno Press, 1979).
5. Matthew Frye Jacobson, *Barbarian Virtues: The United States Encounters Foreign Peoples at Home and Abroad, 1876–1917* (New York: Hill and Wang, 2000), 37–38.
6. Ibid., 33.
7. John W. Dower, *War Without Mercy: Race and Power in the Pacific War* (New York: Pantheon Books, 1986), 155–56.
8. Dyer, *Theodore Roosevelt*, 136–37.
9. Ibid., 137–38.
10. T. Lothrop Stoddard, *The Rising Tide of Color Against White World-Supremacy* (Honolulu: University of Hawaii Press, 2003).
11. Paul Gordon Lauren, "Human Rights in History: Diplomacy and Racial Equality at the Paris Peace Conference," *Diplomatic History* 2 (1978): 257–78.
12. Dower, *War Without Mercy*.
13. Ibid., 78.
14. "How to Tell Your Friends From the Japs," *Time*, December 22, 1941, 33. A similar article, "How to Tell Japs From the Chinese," appeared in *Life*, December 22, 1941, 81–82.
15. "Sax Rohmer (1883–1959)—Original Name Arthur Henry Sarsfield Ward—Wrote Also as Michael Furey," http://www.kirjasto.sci.fi/rohmer.htm (accessed May 8, 2006).

Chapter 4: Black

1. Paul Gordon Lauren, *Power and Prejudice: The Politics and Diplomacy of Racial Discrimination*, 2nd ed. (Boulder: Westview Press, 1996), 224.

2. "Statement of Carlos P. Romulo, Member of the Cabinet, Chairman of the Philippine Delegation to the Asian-African Conference, Bandung, Indonesia," reprinted in Carlos P. Romulo, *The Meaning of Bandung* (Chapel Hill: University of North Carolina Press, 1956), 68–69.

3. Hunt, *Ideology and U.S. Foreign Policy*, 46, 51.

4. Dennis Hickey and Kenneth C. Wylie, *An Enchanting Darkness: The American Vision of Africa in the Twentieth Century* (East Lansing: Michigan State University Press, 1993), 8–13.

5. Ibid., 14.

6. Peter Duignan and L. H. Gann, *The United States and Africa: A History* (Cambridge: Cambridge University Press, 1984), 185, 207.

7. Henry Byroade, "The World's Colonies and Ex-Colonies: A Challenge to America," *State Department Bulletin* 29 (November 16, 1953): 655–60.

8. Seymour M. Hersh, *The Price of Power: Kissinger in the Nixon White House* (New York: Summit Books, 1983): 110–11.

9. Thomas J. Noer, *Cold War and Black Liberation: The United States and White Rule in Africa, 1948–1968* (Columbia: University of Missouri Press, 1985), 30.

10. Michael L. Krenn, *Black Diplomacy: African Americans and the State Department, 1945–1969* (Armonk, NY: M. E. Sharpe, 1999), 88–89.

11. Noer, *Cold War and Black Liberation*, 239–41.

12. Richard Wright, *The Color Curtain: A Report on the Bandung Conference* (Jackson: University Press of Mississippi, 1994), 15, 175–76, 207–8.

13. John D. Silvera, "Color—A Factor in U.S. Psychological Warfare: An Appraisal and Approach to the Use of the Negro as Psywar Themes," *Papers of Dwight D. Eisenhower*, folder 142-B, box 673, Office Files, White House Central Files, Dwight D. Eisenhower Library, Abilene, KS.

14. It should be noted that African-American interest in U.S. foreign relations did not suddenly emerge in the wake of World War II. As a number of studies suggest, this interest extends back to the early nineteenth century. See R. J. M. Blackett, *Building an Antislavery Wall: Black Americans in the Atlantic Abolitionist Movement, 1830–1860* (Baton Rouge: Louisiana State University Press, 1983); Jake C. Miller, *The Black Presence in American Foreign Affairs* (Washington, DC: University Press of America, 1978); Elliott P. Skinner, *African Americans and U.S. Policy Toward Africa, 1850–1924: In Defense of Black National-*

ity (Washington, DC: Howard University Press, 1992); Willard B. Gatewood, *Black Americans and the White Man's Burden, 1898–1903* (Urbana, IL: University of Illinois Press, 1975); Marc Gallicchio, *The African American Encounter With Japan and China: Black Internationalism in Asia, 1895–1945* (Chapel Hill: University of North Carolina Press, 2000); William R. Scott, *The Sons of Sheba's Race: African-Americans and the Italo-Ethiopian War, 1935–1941* (Bloomington: Indiana University Press, 1993).

15. James M. Blaut, "The Theory of Cultural Racism," *Antipode: A Radical Journal of Geography* 23 (1992): 289–99.

16. W. W. Rostow, *The Stages of Economic Growth: A Non-Communist Manifesto* (Cambridge: Cambridge University Press, 1971), 27.

17. Loren Baritz, *Backfire: A History of How American Culture Led Us Into Vietnam and Made Us Fight the Way We Did* (New York: William Morrow and Company, 1985), 129, 177; Michael E. Latham, *Modernization as Ideology: American Social Science and "Nation Building" in the Kennedy Era* (Chapel Hill: University of North Carolina Press, 2000), 196.

18. Latham, *Modernization as Ideology*, 212–13.

19. Peter B. Levy, "Blacks and the Vietnam War," in *The Legacy: The Vietnam War in the American Imagination*, ed. D. Michael Shafer (Boston: Beacon Press, 1990), 211.

20. Full text of the speech is found at http://www.americanrhetoric/com/speeches/mlkatimetobreaksilence.htm.

Conclusion

1. Melani McAlister, *Epic Encounters: Culture, Media, and U.S. Interests in the Middle East, 1945–2000* (Berkeley: University of California Press, 2001), 18–20.

2. Latham, *Modernization as Ideology*, 36–37.

3. Edward W. Said, *Culture and Imperialism* (New York: Vintage Books, 1993), 294–95.

4. McAlister, *Epic Encounters*, 200.

5. Michael L. Krenn, "'America's Face to the World': The Department of State, Arab-Americans, and Diversity in the Wake of 9/11," *The Journal of Gender, Race and Justice* 7:1 (Spring 2003): 150–52.

6. Krenn, "'America's Face to the World,'" 161–65.

SELECTED BIBLIOGRAPHY

Chapter 1: White

Banton, Michael. *Race Relations.* New York: Basic Books, 1967.

Dain, Bruce. *A Hideous Monster of the Mind: American Race Theory in the Early Republic.* Cambridge: Harvard University Press, 2002.

Drinnon, Richard. *Facing West: The Metaphysics of Indian-Hating and Empire-Building.* Norman: University of Oklahoma Press, 1997.

———. "The Metaphysics of Empire-Building: American Imperialism in the Age of Jefferson and Monroe." *The Massachusetts Review* 16 (1975): 666–88.

Gossett, Thomas F. *Race: The History of an Idea in America.* Dallas: Southern Methodist University Press, 1963.

Hanniford, Ivan. *Race: The History of an Idea in the West.* Baltimore: Johns Hopkins University Press, 1996.

Horsman, Reginald. *Josiah Nott of Mobile: Southerner, Physician, and Racial Theorist.* Baton Rouge: Louisiana State University Press, 1987.

———. *Race and Manifest Destiny: The Origins of American Racial Anglo-Saxonism.* Cambridge: Harvard University Press, 1981.

Hunt, Michael H. *Ideology and U.S. Foreign Policy.* New Haven: Yale University Press, 1987.

Jordan, Winthrop D. *The White Man's Burden: Historical Origins of Racism in the United States.* London: Oxford University Press, 1974.

Kaufmann, Eric P. *The Rise and Fall of Anglo-America.* Cambridge: Harvard University Press, 2004.

Nash, Gary B. "Red, White, and Black: The Origins of Racism in Colonial America." In *The Great Fear: Race in the Mind of America*, edited by Gary B. Nash and Richard Weiss, 1–26. New York: Holt, Rinehart and Winston, 1970.

Pearce, Roy Harvey. "The Metaphysics of Indian-Hating." *Ethnohistory* 4 (1957): 27–40.

Thomas, G. E. "Puritans, Indians, and the Concept of Race." *New England Quarterly* 48 (1975): 3–27.

Chapter 2: Brown

Bannister, Robert C. *Social Darwinism: Science and Myth in Anglo-American Social Thought.* Philadelphia: Temple University Press, 1979.

Burton, David. "Theodore Roosevelt's Social Darwinism and Views on Imperialism." *Journal of the History of Ideas* 26 (1965): 103–18.

De León, Arnoldo. *They Called Them Greasers: Anglo Attitudes Toward Mexicans in Texas, 1821–1900.* Austin: University of Texas Press, 1983.

Dyer, Thomas G. *Theodore Roosevelt and the Idea of Race.* Baton Rouge: Louisiana State University Press, 1980.

Gorn, Elliott J. *The Manly Art: Bare-Knuckle Prize Fighting in America.* Ithaca: Cornell University Press, 1986.

Hietala, Thomas R. *Manifest Design: Anxious Aggrandizement in Late Jacksonian America.* Ithaca: Cornell University Press, 1985.

Johnson, John J. *A Hemisphere Apart: The Foundations of United States Policy Toward Latin America.* Baltimore: Johns Hopkins University Press, 1990.

———. *Latin America in Caricature.* Austin: University of Texas Press, 1980.

Kennedy, Philip W. "Race and American Expansion in Cuba and Puerto Rico, 1895–1905." *Journal of Black Studies* 1 (1971): 306–16.

Kenworthy, Eldon. *America/Américas: Myth in the Making of U.S. Policy Toward Latin America.* University Park: Pennsylvania State University Press, 1995.

Lasch, Christopher. "The Anti-Imperialists, the Philippines, and the Inequality of Man." *Journal of Southern History* 24 (1958): 319–31.

Paredes, Raymund A. "The Origins of Anti-Mexican Sentiment in the United States." In *New Directions in Chicano Scholarship*, edited by Ricardo Romo and Raymund A. Paredes, 139–65. La Jolla: University of California at San Diego Press, 1978.

Park, James William. *Latin American Underdevelopment: A History of Perspectives in the United States, 1870–1965.* Baton Rouge: Louisiana State University Press, 1995.

Pike, Fredrick B. *The United States and Latin America: Myths and Stereotypes of Civilization and Nature.* Austin: University of Texas Press, 1992.

Rydell, Robert W. *All the World's a Fair: Visions of Empire at American International Expositions, 1876–1916.* Chicago: University of Chicago Press, 1984.

Weber, David J. "'Scarce More Than Apes': Historical Roots of Anglo American Stereotypes of Mexicans in the Border Region." In *New Spain's Far Northern Frontier: Essays on Spain in the New West, 1540–1821*, 295–307. Albuquerque: University of New Mexico Press, 1979.

Weinberg, Albert K. *Manifest Destiny: A Study of Nationalist Expansionism in American History.* Baltimore: Johns Hopkins University Press, 1935.

Weston, Rubin Francis. *Racism in U.S. Imperialism: The Influence of Racial Assumptions on American Foreign Policy, 1893–1946.* Columbia: University of South Carolina Press, 1972.

Chapter 3: Yellow

Dower, John W. *War Without Mercy: Race and Power in the Pacific War.* New York: Pantheon Books, 1986.

Dyer, Thomas G. *Theodore Roosevelt and the Idea of Race.* Baton Rouge: Louisiana State University Press, 1980.

Gallicchio, Marc. *The African American Encounter With Japan and China: Black Internationalism in Asia, 1895–1945.* Chapel Hill: University of North Carolina Press, 2000.

Hunt, Michael H. *Ideology and U.S. Foreign Policy.* New Haven: Yale University Press, 1987.

Iriye, Akira. *Across the Pacific: An Inner History of American—East Asian Relations.* New York: Harcourt Brace and World, 1967.

Jacobson, Matthew Frye. *Barbarian Virtues: The United States Encounters Foreign Peoples at Home and Abroad, 1876–1917.* New York: Hill and Wang, 2000.

Lauren, Paul Gordon. "Human Rights in History: Diplomacy and Racial Equality at the Paris Peace Conference." *Diplomatic History* 2 (1978): 257–78.

Miller, Stuart Creighton. "The American Trader's Image of China, 1785–1840." *Pacific Historical Review* 36 (1967): 375–95.

———. *The Unwelcome Immigrant: The American Image of the Chinese, 1785–1882.* Berkeley: University of California Press, 1969.

Minear, Richard H. "Cross-Cultural Perceptions and World War II: American Japanists of the 1940s and Their Images of Japan." *International Studies Quarterly* 24 (1980): 555–80.

Spoehr, Luther W. "Sambo and the Heathen Chinee: Californians' Racial Stereotypes in the Late 1870s." *Pacific Historical Review* 42 (1973): 185–204.

Thorne, Christopher. "Racial Aspects of the Far Eastern War of 1941–1945." *Proceedings of the British Academy* 66 (1980): 329–77.

Chapter 4: Black

Anderson, Carol. *Eyes off the Prize: The United Nations and the African American Struggle for Human Rights, 1944–1955*. Cambridge: Cambridge University Press, 2003.

Barkan, Elazar. *The Retreat of Scientific Racism: Changing Concepts of Race in Britain and the United States Between the World Wars*. Cambridge: Cambridge University Press, 1992.

Blaut, James M. "The Theory of Cultural Racism." *Antipode: A Radical Journal of Geography* 23 (1992): 289–99.

Borstelmann, Thomas. *Apartheid's Reluctant Uncle: The United States and South Africa in the Early Cold War*. New York: Oxford University Press, 1993.

———. *The Cold War and the Color Line: American Race Relations in the Global Arena*. Cambridge: Harvard University Press, 2003.

Dudziak, Mary L. *Cold War Civil Rights: Race and the Image of American Democracy*. Princeton: Princeton University Press, 2002.

Duignan, Peter, and L. H. Gann. *The United States and Africa: A History*. Cambridge: Cambridge University Press, 1984.

Engerman, David, Nils Gilman, Mark Haefele, and Michael E. Latham, eds. *Staging Growth: Modernization, Development, and the Global Cold War*. Amherst: University of Massachusetts Press, 2003.

Fairclough, Adam. "Martin Luther King, Jr. and the War in Vietnam." *Phylon* 45 (1984): 19–39.

Gilman, Nils. *Mandarins of the Future: Modernization Theory in Cold War America*. Baltimore: Johns Hopkins University Press, 2003.

Hersh, Seymour M. *The Price of Power: Kissinger in the Nixon White House*. New York: Summit Books, 1983.

Hickey, Dennis, and Kenneth C. Wylie. *An Enchanting Darkness: The American Vision of Africa in the Twentieth Century*. East Lansing: Michigan State University Press, 1993.

Krenn, Michael L. *Black Diplomacy: African Americans and the State Department, 1945–1969*. Armonk, NY: M. E. Sharpe, 1999.

———. "'Unfinished Business': Segregation and U.S. Diplomacy at the 1958 World's Fair." *Diplomatic History* 20:4 (Fall 1996): 591–612.

Lauren, Paul Gordon. *Power and Prejudice: The Politics and Diplomacy of Racial Discrimination*, 2nd ed. Boulder: Westview Press, 1996.

Latham, Michael E. *Modernization as Ideology: American Social Science and "Nation Building" in the Kennedy Era*. Chapel Hill: University of North Carolina Press, 2000.

Levy, Peter B. "Blacks and the Vietnam War." In *The Legacy: The Vietnam War in the American Imagination*, edited by D. Michael Shafer, 209–32. Boston: Beacon Press, 1990.

Metz, Stephen. "Congress, the Antiapartheid Movement, and Nixon." *Diplomatic History* 12 (1988): 165–85.

Noer, Thomas J. *Cold War and Black Liberation: The United States and White Rule in Africa, 1948–1968.* Columbia: University of Missouri Press, 1985.

Plummer, Brenda Gayle. *Rising Wind: Black Americans and U.S. Foreign Affairs, 1935–1960.* Chapel Hill: University of North Carolina Press, 1996.

Romulo, Carlos P. *The Meaning of Bandung.* Chapel Hill: University of North Carolina Press, 1956.

Wright, Richard. *The Color Curtain: A Report on the Bandung Conference.* Jackson: University Press of Mississippi, 1994.

Conclusion

Krenn, Michael L. "'America's Face to the World': The Department of State, Arab-Americans, and Diversity in the Wake of 9/11." *The Journal of Gender, Race and Justice* 7:1 (Spring 2003): 149–66.

McAlister, Melani. *Epic Encounters: Culture, Media, and U.S. Interests in the Middle East, 1945–2000.* Berkeley: University of California Press, 2001.

Said, Edward W. *Culture and Imperialism.* New York: Vintage Books, 1993.

INDEX

ABOUT THE AUTHOR

MICHAEL L. KRENN is a professor of history and the chair of the department at Appalachian State University and the author of several books, including *Black Diplomacy: African-Americans and the State Department, 1945–1969* and *Fall-Out Shelters for the Human Spirit: American Art and the Cold War.* He lives in Boone, North Carolina.